# WALKING BACK
# TO HAPPINESS

# WALKING BACK TO HAPPINESS

## TALES OF WALKING FOOTBALLERS

STEVE BATCHELOR

In association with Phil Andrews & 'the players' of
Moulton Masters Walking Football Club, Northampton, England

FIRST EDITION

978-1-80227-518-6 (paperback)

978-1-80227-519-3 (ebook)

Prepared by PublishingPush.com

"We don't stop playing because we grow old, we grow old because we stop playing!"

George Bernard Shaw

# Preface

The rise of the curious new sport of Walking Football in recent years has been phenomenal, with over 1,500 new clubs being formed in England and by now, probably more than one hundred thousand new players taking part.

The sport is truly all inclusive and admits players of all abilities regardless of age, size, gender, disability, colour or creed.

This book tells the story of one man's vision combined with the tales of a bunch of ordinary men and one brave woman, who make up around 20% of the total membership of our marvellous club.

It embraces terrible circumstances as players speak openly of their problems with injury and illnesses, including surviving a life threatening car crash, and living with cancer and diabetes.

The book confronts issues of obesity, loneliness and depression caused by bereavement or loss of employment, yet despite many truly sad stories the book manages to be quite joyous and uplifting as the warmth of human spirit is spread through something as simple as playing football at a walking pace...

Steve Batchelor, age 72
Moulton Master walking footballer, October 2021

# Index of Contributors

# Additional material

Walking Football & mental health

Moulton Masters honours & achievements

Beginners guide to Walking Football

Community activities & friendship groups

Reflections by Phil Andrews

# CHAPTER 1

# Phil Andrews (Club founder)

The surgeon stood at the bottom of my bed and now was the nerve-wracking moment of truth. I'd been 'in theatre' for seven hours, and now it was time for the prognosis. I'd looked down as soon as I'd awoken and had been relieved to see both my feet, so I was thankful I'd not lost a leg or two. Twenty four hours earlier I'd been warned by a paramedic not to look down at my legs – but then the desire to 'check the damage' was too great. At that moment I could not feel either leg; the left was wedged in the footwell, whilst the right had one too many angles in it – I sat there pinned in my vehicle for 90 minutes, and resigned to losing one or both as I was winched out of the roof by the Fire & Rescue team.

Now, the small-built Sri Lankan consultant, who was to become 'my friend and rock,' uttered those words – *'I'm sorry, there was too much damage …. you will never play football again as you won't be able to take any impact,"* but, he beamed, *"you will be able to walk."*

I was 49 years and 7 months old, and my aim that year was to be playing football at the 50+ milestone as had Stanley Matthews (albeit I was a much lower standard!).

I had been playing football all my life as a hobby and now it was suddenly over. OK, I'd been lucky to be playing that long but had kept myself super-fit, having spent 16 years in the Military, which I'd left 10 years before. And I hadn't had a serious injury except an ACL (Anterior Cruciate Ligament) and a bout of PTSD (Post Traumatic Stress Disorder). However, maybe it was the morphine, or his kindly tone, but I was just so relieved to hear that I'd be able to walk again, that I could hopefully resign myself to playing no more football, or maybe become a goalkeeper? Although, there was another sting for me - I wouldn't be able to walk uphill or on uneven ground – so no more hill-trekking – which had just become my other great passion.

The previous Easter I'd climbed one of the toughest fells in the Lake District, the Fairfield Horseshoe; now my dreams of walking up Scafell, the 127-mile coast-to-coast or the Pennine Way were over... and all because some bloke was in a rush to get home and tried to overtake five cars at the same time and hit me smack head-on, on a country lane that cold, drizzly February evening!

That crash (the emergency services quite rightly now don't call them an 'accident' as they're not – it's usually someone's fault) was in 2007.

Eight years later, my marriage of 30 years had collapsed under the stress and strain of my life-changing injuries. I'd had to resign from the job I'd loved as a fraud investigator (as I couldn't face the hours driving all over the country). I'd then failed to cope with office-bound jobs I tried, and unsurprisingly, I had a recurrence of my PTSD (I'd originally suffered from it a year after the first Gulf War). Now I wasn't finding life that appealing, and had failed to form new relationships. My recuperation was taking years – I had other subsequent major operations, including one on my tibial nerve to regain more feeling, and another to strengthen the right ankle which cost me mid-foot flexibility, as I had to have it pinned.

My military training certainly helped my determination to regain as much fitness as I could. In total I undertook over 1,000 hours of physiotherapy and had built up my strength and stamina enough to prove one thing wrong to my surgeon – I managed to climb a mountain again – Haystacks; the summit was the burial site of Arthur Wainwright, the noted Cumbrian fell-walker and author. I am eternally grateful for this to my old school friend, Richard Watson, who had moved to Cumbria in the eighties and was now a seasoned local walking-guide. But, although I could sort of run with a heavy limp, any sport was out of the question.

Suggestions were made including racket sports, but I tried and failed; golf and archery were non-starters as my back was weakened by the months in a wheelchair or on crutches (for which I'm now awaiting a stent operation on my weakened spine). Indoor 10-pin bowling didn't work either, and I wasn't a lover of swimming due to it being solitary and boring, although I did find that at least it would build up my strength.

By chance, sometime in 2015 I had bumped into a long-lost teammate from the late seventies who was about to change my life with a few words:

*"Hey Phil, heard of that new sport that's been invented just for you?"* My friend, Steve Parker, added that it was 'Walking Football' and had been used in a TV advert by Barclays Bank a couple of years before to assist the silver generation with the digital age with things such as on-line banking. This drew a blank stare from me but he said it had transformed his life, and even with 'his knees' he could now play in goal. Steve had been a brilliant centre-forward in his day (his cousin was Keith Berschin of Ipswich, Birmingham City and England B fame) and had been knocking in hat-tricks for our Sunday team every week; unfortunately we always let in four or more, so we never won; that was, until Steve dropped back into defence and then we didn't concede! Unfortunately, without his goals we still failed to win until we eventually found a winning formula.

Some time later I suddenly remembered this suggestion of Steve's and thought I'd pop along to watch him play at nearby Towcester Leisure Centre. I was soon roped into playing and was assured I'd be well-looked after, and they were right - I loved it; however, it was quite a drive to the venue. I tried a few other closer venues and always found them very welcoming. However, none were quite right for me:

One group was so short of numbers that they'd introduced this 'bring your son along,' and a couple of those remained and wanted to showboat, and even dominate games; another was a bit cliquey, and all the originals were mates whilst all the newbies were thrown together into one team and never gelled or progressed, so lost every week. The nearest one was indoors and this caused pains to my joints, while another was on grass, and they only played in the evening when it was too slippery for me. Some pitches were so small that not everyone could fit on and we took turns watching from the side-lines which was frustrating, and with my muscles needing extra time to warm up I got strains and sprains due to them cooling down. Some venues didn't want to play ALL the rules, so they would allow running as it was too difficult to define walking, while others introduced three touches to combat running – which some guys found too restrictive as they just couldn't control the ball after four touches, let alone 3! Some venues allowed the ball over head height – again as no-one could define it, others were a bit elitist and only wanted 'proper footballers' – that's me out then! One had a hardman who relished welcoming new players with a thumping tackle; when he illegally slid in on me, putting me out for the rest of the session, and the referee ignored it, I thought maybe this sport wasn't for me. But please don't let my experience put you off! I was being super-critical at this time of my life.

I felt like Goldilocks!! and needed a club that was 'exactly right' for me but knew I had n't yet found it. I discovered via social media there were Walking Football clubs opening up all over the country, but most argued about the rules and how to implement them.

So, only one solution – start my own club and we would follow the proper rules! It would be football for all, and we would accept anyone who turned up to play.

This was the least daunting aspect of the whole thing as I'd previously formed a football club in my early twenties with mates like Steve Parker who I mentioned above, and I'd organised a couple of sporting events in the Civil Service, then numerous ones in both the Army and RAF (yes, long story but I was in both!). However, I soon found a guy who had a pair of goals and a ball, and he knew of a nice piece of flat grass (This was Sileby Rangers FC car park in Moulton which is on the north east side of Northampton). It was available on a Friday morning which was an ideal day to start, and we chose 11am to kick off so that any dew was dried off. I then needed to 'badger' a few older footie mates to come along and try it out. Most were from the Supporters Bar at Northampton Town FC named Carr's Bar (after our successful manager in the mid-eighties, and father of locally born comedian Alan Carr), and a few had heard of the sport and wanted to try it out. I got busy on Facebook and contacted all my friends to tell everyone else; some were indignant saying they were much too young, so I said to tell their dads or Grandads!

So, five of us started and one brought his dog, Gnasher, who we allowed to play until he dominated the game so we had to sin-bin him to his dad's car. Everyone loved it, so we agreed we'd all work on finding a mate or two to bring. We charged a couple of quid for the hour and eventually there was enough cash to buy our own 'pop-up' goals, a ball, and some bibs.

Around this time, I was doing some research into the origin of the sport and found an article which mentioned that a John Croot had invented it at Chesterfield , which is well-covered in other books. Another was Colin Dolan, who is now MD of Liverpool Football Therapy. (I think he's an Everton fan) and he had contacted fellow Toffee-fan, Andy Burnham, who is currently Mayor of Manchester, but I recall that Andy had just stepped down as Shadow Home Secretary, was a former Secretary of State for Health and also for Sport. Colin and Andy co-chaired a conference at the Palace of Westminster (now there's an impressive building!) which I managed to obtain an invitation to, that featured some amateur footballers who admitted that playing football had saved their lives. They'd made suicide attempts and it was quite a distressing tale. One of the last speakers was former professional footballer, Andy Woodward, who had recently hit the national headlines as the whistle-blower for the sexual abuse he had suffered as a child at the hands of a football coach who was later convicted of being a paedophile. The evening was very inspirational for me, and galvanised my mind-set and concentrated my thoughts into what I imagined the club ethos should be – my club would be 'football for all' and banned would be the former 'prima-donnas' who had blighted the lives of many youngsters by missing training, but then turning up at 2 minutes before kick-off, so yours truly was dropped to the subs bench. It's sad there are still a few prima-donnas around even now at 60, thinking they can just walk into a team and instantly play instead of a lesser, but longer-serving player, who helps run the club.

During the autumn with the damp ground, we decided to move indoors to play in a sports centre and of course that day was the sunniest in weeks and some wanted to play outdoors; likewise we moved outdoors in Spring, and it was the wettest day! Some joker of course said *"Can't we play indoors!?"* The next summer we couldn't play at Sileby so we decided to tour the town to where we used to play as kids and see if any pitch was suitable for a 'home venue', preferably near a pub. We even thought we'd ask the local 'friends of the park ' to try and stir up some more interest, but mostly this failed – word of mouth was still the best way to grow. So, we re-lived our youth playing at these 'grounds': Abington Park (by the bandstand), The Racecourse, the Recs at Kingsthorpe, and Far Cotton, Dallington, other parks at Errington, Wootton, Hunsbury, Hardingstone, Eastfield.

One of our regulars was a Liverpudlian, Terry Marconi, who didn't know the town and lived in a village nearby. Feeling sorry for dragging him all over town, we descended on his local village playing field; shame the farmer hadn't cleared the 'green' as we played amongst the cut grass that was turning into straw. However, having a nice village pub to retreat to was heaven.

Meanwhile, all of us knew of a few 'younger guys' in their fifties who were interested in 'having a go' but they still worked. So, as I was now fitter and felt I could play twice a week, I looked around and found that Moulton School Sports Centre (Pound Lane) had an all-weather sand-based 2G Hockey pitch for hire under floodlights.

So, starting with just eight of us including one guy roped into playing in his best suit and shoes after coming from work just to look, we started our Monday evening session. However, numbers didn't grow until we moved to an all-weather surface at a more central venue at Malcolm Arnold Academy. However, it quickly became too cramped with 9 a side so we returned to Moulton School, where we routinely had 9-a-side for weeks on a bigger pitch.

However, it was sad, but we found that sometimes the keenest guys were often those who had had to retire due to injury and neither indoors, grass or this hard sand-based Astro-turf was conducive to their injuries - they had to retire again, or restrict themselves to playing only fortnightly at most. We played there for a year or more in sun, wind, rain, and snow! What was needed was a 3G all-weather pitch which has more 'give' in the surface.

When driving around town I had assumed that at least one of the unused Astroturf pitches I could see could be hired out to us for an hour; although it would cost us a bit more, it would be a simple choice of which one was best. However, I was aghast to discover that all eighteen were 'each owned' by a local school and therefore could not be used by adults. Even the most expensive 'Goals' commercial facility was part of Abbeyfield school. A local firm of solicitors had one at Riverside Business Park but wouldn't let us play on it. I couldn't believe this and discussed it with the council who directed me towards the unused facility at Kings Heath. Sadly, in two minutes we could see why – they'd spent £1000s on the pitch and floodlighting but only about twenty quid on security - a chain-link fence which the local tear-aways had pulled apart and were using the pitch as a bike park. There were ripped up areas and the rest was covered in moss, although an associate of mine said he could approach local businesspeople for funding to repair it. However, it would need a full-time guard or caretaker and no way could we consider that for just our two hours a week. Five years later it still remains dormant, unused, unloved and a total waste of taxpayers' money.

We asked the local FA if there were any facilities being considered and learnt there was one, but they wouldn't tell us where it was or who owned it! Then quite by chance one member heard that it was next-door to our home - at Moulton FC, and we moved in September 2018! This was surely written in the stars; there was a strong connection here with the same Steve Parker who had first told me about the sport over 3 years before. His Dad, Fred Parker, had been first team manager there in the seventies, I had played with Steve a few times in the Sunday league – through my working with his brother, Mike. Then the brothers had joined my ex-school team when I formed it in 1978. When the Chairman of Moulton FC interviewed us, he said they'd tried to start their own Walking Football club here with little success and I discovered that had been tried by the same Steve Parker I knew! So, the final chapter was we moved in, and I can never see us playing anywhere else - who wouldn't want to play here?

In 2015, when I first visited all those other local Walking Football set-ups to try them out, the thing which really struck me at all of them was how much you miss the 'dressing-room' banter. Although, there was often no room it was the arrival place to get changed. "Here comes Joe, late again, get here when you can," "Wouldn't she let you out, she hid your kit?;" "Told her you've popped out for a bottle of milk and a paper?", "Won't she spot you've been playing again?" "Nah! He never breaks into a sweat , he doesn't move fast enough to work up a sweat"; "He'll sweat more when she asks where the milk is!".

Now, Joe has probably never been late before but because of this once, he gets full barrels from his new teammates, and he loves it! It makes him feel he's part of a group and he'll ensure he's not last next time. We have a guy, John Mulcahy, who is always late and as we expanded and more Johns joined, he became known as 'Late John.' That worked well until one day we were discussing him to a new guy, and yes, he thought someone had died!

Then, with COVID-19 rules we had to start locking the gate, so John HAD to turn up on time, and we needed a new nickname.

Post lockdown and the restrictions were lifted, John fell into his previous habits and turned up late again. However, inadvertently we might have stumbled on a cure for him - one night he had to ring a teammate who was on his way home, and get him to return and let him out of the locked changing room! Those of us in the bar had not heard him calling or ringing us! We placated him by saying as he was playing the session on the following morning at least he wouldn't been late for that – he didn't quite see the funny side of it!

As I'm a bit of a social butterfly I really enjoy the recruitment side of the job. Not knowing who the next member will be, everyone springs a surprise. When someone brings a mate, you often get a mini-CV from them of their playing experience, work, ability, fitness, injury, and there must always be a reference as to whether he's a good bloke or not. He may be a gifted player, ex-semi-pro, but if he can't gel with the rest of the guys, we may not pursue his recruitment. Guys usually know if they fit in with the crowd and if not, they move on to the next club. However, this is rare, but we don't care: if you were Ibrahimovic himself, you'll still possibly not get the full welcome at our club if you don't fit in with the other guys.

We have top blokes in our club, all helping each other on and off the pitch. The better players help the less able enormously and the standard of all has improved, so much so that I would struggle to get in to my own club if I joined now! Our 'more able' guys realise that without 'the others' there wouldn't be enough payers to have a match, so they don't mind when the odd pass strays, or there's a wayward shot, for the bigger picture of having a great inclusive club, and avoiding cliques. At the end of the day a shot is a shot, and the fact that a chance is created is normally enough for the team. We are not particularly bothered about scores – well a few are, and probably keep a record somewhere, I'm told – but we get far more enjoyment out of Joe's shot that trickled over the line, as he has a debilitating disease, or has fought back against horrendous injuries, than Billy Whizz who notched another hat-trick.

However, there was much to be said about the positivity of COVID-19 in that OK, we couldn't mix, so we stayed in our bubbles of six for some drills. We decided to keep the same bubbles all session, then when allowed we played against another six.

Now, we are back to our pre-COVID rules of teams of six playing in a round-robin format mixing everyone of varying abilities and fitness levels. However, COVID also made everyone realise how much they needed the sessions; they depended on the social interaction, albeit restricted. They were also furloughed or working from home so had nowhere else to go! Consequently, our numbers dramatically increased, and we had enough for six teams instead of four. So, the fitter, younger guys played a round-robin, leaving us less fit guys playing another match. This divides the session quite nicely, as the slower guys now get far more time on the ball and feel happier that they won't get closed down so quickly or tackled so hard. However, the downside is they don't get so much coaching to improve their own game. A mixture of both ideas will now prevail

The pitches and facilities at Moulton FC...

When making notes for this book I was ruminating on my previous playing 'career' and it was an interesting bit of research summarised below:

**1968**: Weston Favell County Primary School – Couldn't get in the A or B team, but played for hours after school, weekends and holidays.

**c1973**: Yellow Sabbath (Sunday team from Rugby-playing Boys Grammar School, originally formed just to 'take on' Red Star, formed by Ken Scott) from the same school year. We next met again until 45 years later playing Walking Football..!

**c1977**: Strollers, Moulton FC* (yes, played a few times, then I coincidentally re-joined the same club 41 years later!)

**1978**: Founded Riverside (Ex NGS boys)

**1980-1996**: Various Army teams in Hong Kong, Germany and RAF Wyton.

**1996-2007**: 'Organiser' for Monday night Travis Perkins kickabout.

**2015**: Founded this Walking Football Club as "Northampton Town FC Fans", then "Northampton WF."

**2018**: Re-named the group as Moulton Masters when we joined Moulton FC (founded 1896) who had teams from aged 6 (boys and girls) through to youth, men's, vets and ladies.

Thus, you can now join the club aged 5 and never leave!

Steve Batchelor

# CHAPTER 2

# Steve Batchelor

I moved between two defenders as I received the ball from the wing; turning, I faced the centre back and could see my teammate advancing toward the edge of the penalty area to my right. I feigned to pass but instead swivelled and drove the ball with my left foot directly into the bottom corner of the goal from 15 yards, with their goalkeeper flat footed.

"Fuck me, he's scored with his left peg," said Derek.

"Jammy bastard," grumbled Dave, one of the opposition defenders.

"It was a toe poke," smiled Jim and he approached and then almost imperceptibly mumbled, "nice finish".

No, this wasn't a match to decide a European championship or a play-off final – just a Monday night training game between a bunch of ageing men, all over fifty and mostly overweight, and all playing the phenomenal new sport of 'Walking Football'

I had recently passed my 70th birthday and the reason for the good-natured ribbing was due to the fact I was shortly to attend a trial for the England over 70's National team and the humorous derision at my exploits was all part of the dressing room banter that everyone in our team felt was lost forever when our days of playing 'proper' football had passed several decades earlier...

When I added another goal with a right foot in the second half many of my team-mates conceded that the recent quality of my finishing was possibly slightly above average for such an old bloke, but the barbed comments continued - although always with a smile, and in dressing room parlance, sometimes just being called 'an annoying tosser' can be received as a compliment...

No-one cared that my team actually lost the match, 6-3 or that 'Deano' had bagged a hat-trick for the opposition, or that we were playing a game of football on officially the hottest August day on record – no, I had become the subject of tonight's banter due entirely to the impending England trial and I just had to grin and bear it...!

Despite doing well in the trials, I didn't make the final cut, although I was eventually invited back for future trials. Fortunately our excellent goalkeeper, Dave Poole, did get selected but had to wait until the lockdown break in August 2020 to finally win his first cap – much to the great delight of everyone associated with Moulton Masters WFC...

My own exploits continued throughout 2019 and were crowned by being part of Moulton Masters over 65's tournament winning team, and featuring in the early formation of our over 70's team as I still continued to play twice weekly with my growing number of friends at this marvellous club.

Sadly, my England ambitions came to a grinding halt when Covid-19 struck and we were all forced into lockdown and a frustrating year of growing older, and another bout of health problems meant I would be happy to just be playing again.

When, finally, we did return in March 2021 I was compelled to play in the (slightly) less competitive 'old codgers' games which were basically friendlies amongst the same group of 14-20 players with teams shuffled around to keep things interesting. This game was extremely useful for new members learning the ropes, players of any standard returning from injury or illness and of course, some of us more advanced in years who simply needed a slower paced game. Somewhat embarrassingly, but also awfully good for my ego, was the fact that I suddenly became a key striker in these games and due to a combination of slightly slower defenders, stand-in goalies and a great deal of good fortune I was able to accumulate a lot of goals in these games and suddenly my latest health problems didn't seem to matter so much...

## A new beginning

I had discovered the many benefits of Walking Football in April 2018, having seen the diminutive BBC sports reporter, Mike Bushel, give it a go during a TV news bulletin. Curious at how simple this looked I researched it further on the internet and then thought it looked utterly ridiculous – basically just a bunch of fat and bald old men kicking a ball about with no real purpose or passion.

However, having continued to investigate it further I became intrigued by the many benefits it claimed to give participants, particularly with regard to regular exercise and companionship, both of which were sadly missing in my life at the time.

I searched for local teams but was disappointed to find my nearest was in Peterborough, not a place I was particularly fond of, not least because it was a boring 60 minute drive from where I lived in Northampton - so I abandoned the idea.

I had last played 'proper' football in my late thirties although I did have a minor renaissance in 2013 when I played with a bunch of neighbours on the local artificial pitch, having been invited by the local vicar who was also a personal friend. "Come and have a kick about; most of the blokes are over forty," he said – so I did, and although I found the pace unrelenting, I was pleased that I could still pass the ball and even score the odd goal, but it was apparent that I was easily the oldest one there and as such, some of the younger ones – who were actually in their 20's and 30's -did make allowances for me and held back from some of the more robust tackling.

All was going well, with 'the lads' meeting every Tuesday evening and gradually the numbers began to swell, and the ages of the participants grew younger, and the matches became fiercer - until one week when I was tackled by a particularly athletic guy near the wire fence that enclosed the pitch, and as I fell he landed on me, with his elbow cracking my ribs.

I had previously broken ribs in a fracas some years ago so after this latest episode I was well aware that the hospital could offer no real treatment, but nonetheless went for an X-ray just to ensure no further damage had been done.

The doctor seemed surprised when she asked how I had managed to break my ribs and I explained I had been playing football – "How old are you Mr Batchelor" she said; "63 last birthday," I replied. "I think it's time you hung up your boots," she warned me with a smile, then went on to explain that if this happened again it could be quite serious.

An X-ray had revealed scarring to my left lung that was defined as an elevated hemidiaphragm and I was advised to avoid contact sports and so, on that day I resigned myself to the fact I would never play football again...

I had suffered severe asthma as a child and was so unwell I had trouble even climbing the stairs. Eventually my condition improved to an extent that I was able to run and swim like other children, but I was 11 years old before I could kick a football with any meaning.

However, by the time I was 16 I was captain and centre forward for my school team and had even been noticed by scouts at Reading FC where I played in a trial against such notables as Maurice Evans and Jimmy Wheeler.

My real ambition of course was to play for my family team, Queens Park Rangers, but I figured Reading might have to do for now, and at least they also played in blue and white hoops!

Like many other young boys with a footballing dream I subsequently never made the grade, but was quite happy turning out for a succession of local North West London amateur teams on Saturday afternoons and Sunday mornings for the next 20 years, and then retired aged 38.

The highlights of my footballing life were being a spectator at Wembley supporting England in 1966 and then, only nine months later, being a supporter at Wembley as Queens Park Rangers triumphed in the 1967 League Cup Final.

I subsequently wrote a book about my exploits during the 1966 World Cup, imaginatively entitled, 'I was there in '66'.

As this is still available from Amazon many of my Moulton Masters teammates got hold of a copy and provided the encouragement and inspiration for me to put this book together on their behalf, and this has been a true labour of love.

After retiring from playing football aged 38, I then decided to take up distance running with an ambition to complete the London Marathon which I managed to achieve in 1988 in a time of 3 hours 50 minutes, and I also competed in numerous half marathons.

I was employed as a Director of a Ventilation Company and worked mainly in North London, but moved to Northampton to take a senior post with a Swedish Company in early 2001, and in 2009 I formed my own business designing, supplying and installing ventilation systems.

Sadly, my life fell apart in 2016 when my partner for the past ten years fell ill with leukaemia and one of my trusted employees decided to embezzle my business as I was away from work at the hospital so much of the time.

The net result of this situation was my girlfriend died after 11 months of suffering this terrible illness, my business was forced into liquidation, and I was compelled to sell my house to clear my debts and avoid becoming bankrupt.

Although I had divorced in 2003, I had custody of my youngest daughter who was by then studying to go to university, so although I was in the depths of depression I had to carry on for her sake and decided to restart my business, but without staff or overheads, and concentrate on consultancy work only, and this very quickly became quite successful.

However, something was missing from my life as my year of misery had left me avoiding all social contact and I was becoming very unfit – it was then I discovered the joys of Walking Football, having first met Phil Andrews at Danes Camp Leisure Centre, where we played 4 a side indoors on a noisy and sweaty basketball court.

Immediately I was hooked and soon began to take it more and more seriously which is where my story began...

Today I am content as I have re-established family life with my ex-wife from 20 years ago and am being kept busier than ever thanks to the Government constantly advertising for me that 'good ventilation is the key to controlling Covid'.

My football is not quite to the standard of a couple of years ago due to the onset of illness and old age but this doesn't diminish my enjoyment at all, and I still play the way I like to, much to the amusement or frustration of others depending what team they are in – yes, it's great to nutmeg someone (especially Dave H) and be called an 'annoying tosser' – long may it continue...

# CHAPTER 3

# Billy Horne - Tribute

It was inevitable that eventually our group would lose someone to the ravages of illness or old age, and the first player to leave the pitch forever was Billy Horne
    England & Moulton over 70's goalkeeper, Dave Poole takes up the story...
    It was at a mutual friend's funeral when I asked Billy to join Moulton Masters. Though I had never played in the same team as him, only against him, there was no doubt in my mind he would become a great asset to the club with his special abilities. From day one, Billy embraced Walking Football for what it is all about - no levels, everyone playing regardless of gender, age and/or ability. I can still hear him now shouting encouragement 'great ball, lovely pass, well hit and super save'.
    Regardless of whether he was playing or watching Billy would always encourage others. I think Billy was made to manage our over 70's side and I, for one, benefited from his support and encouragement. Off the pitch, Billy's jovial and friendly nature shone through - when we could finally get him out of the changing room as Bill was always the last man out...
    I think I can speak for Ian, Ron, John, Alan and the rest of the team in saying he was a big part of our Tuesday and Friday sessions. That cup of coffee

and time together, putting the world to rights and reliving the past. Billy always had a joke on his phone and would often talk about his time at Rushden Town and Northampton Spencer. Well, that's if I would let him get a word in. Super memories.

Billy was a highly regarded local footballer and many will have their memories of the floppy, ginger-haired forward with the sweet left foot. Especially defenders who had been nutmegged or left on their backside by Billy's undoubted skill. Though I remember him in his prime, probably my most cherished memories are from more recent times at Moulton Masters, some tinged with sadness but mainly uplifting and joyful.

God Bless Billy. A true gentleman, a gifted footballer and a loyal friend – you are sorely missed...

Editor's note: Billy suffered with serious injuries throughout his time with Moulton Masters but he would still turn up each week and get changed and insist on paying his 'subs' before practising on his own. He would act as the oldest ball boy in town and would be shouting encouragement from the touchline before asking politely if he could join in for the last 15 minutes and then invariably impress us with an astute pass or the occasional goal.

He would then stay until the end of each session, simply because he loved to chat....

# CHAPTER 4

# Dave Poole

Our Manager, Phil Andrews, informed me that England were holding trials for over 70's and would I be interested? Steve Batchelor had some more details about it, and I decided 'why not' and gave Steve a call.

There were 3 venues: Sheffield, Romford and Weston-Super-Mare. After talking with Steve, we both agreed that Romford would be the one for us and luckily for me Steve offered to drive us there.

On the day of the trials my wife dropped me at Steve's for the journey to Romford. On our way down Steve and I both agreed it was more of an adventure than expecting to be picked, and a good opportunity to assess ourselves against other players with similar aspirations.

As for the trials themselves, we were split into 8 teams of 2 sections. Steve and I were in different sections which seemed to work out quite well as, when I wasn't playing, I could watch Steve and vice versa.

As for my own performances, they were OK and resulted in the manager telling me afterwards that they had marked me as second keeper on the day, noting that I had done better than other 'keepers in the Sheffield trial, but I must now wait for the outcome of the West Country trials.

As for Steve I was convinced he would get into the squad. He managed to score in every game and his last game was the best on the day. I actually saw the whole match, and, in my opinion, Steve was the best player on the pitch. At our next session at Moulton Masters, people were asking how Steve and I got on...For me, I told them what the manager had said and that I was convinced Steve would be in the squad that was to be announced in October prior to the game against Wales. I thought that even if I did make the squad I might not be able to play as I was only 69 and the trials were to get a squad together for the European championship in 2020. Sadly, neither Steve nor I made the squad but the disappointment was tempered by the manager asking whether we would be prepared to trial again after the Wales game in November. I agreed, and I believe Steve agreed as well. So, you can imagine my surprise when I received an email a few days later asking for my availability to play in a squad game in Birmingham. I jumped at the chance and three managers later I'm still in the England squad, winning four caps to date and hoping one day to surpass Peter Shilton's record...

So now at the age of 70 I can proudly say I am an England International Footballer, and my family and teammates are all chuffed to bits by my selection. It is just a shame that Covid put paid to the planned 2020 European Championships. Still, there's always the next Walking Football world cup to aspire to...

Editor's note (Phil Andrews): At Dave's second trial I offered to drive him to Sutton Coldfield as I knew he would be nervous.

When chatting to the England Manager I found myself being asked to referee. Apparently, Steve Batchelor had told him that a number of Moulton Masters players had taken a Walking Football referee's course and he had even reffed some of the Romford trial games (when he wasn't playing). So, I gladly accepted, and all seemed to go so well that at the next England get together we had a couple more of our guys, Mark Simpson and Dean Barron, along to support Dave and they too found themselves officiating!

What a day it was for our little club with everyone 'mucking in' to give the older guys another day to live the dream.

# CHAPTER 5

# Len Driver

I chatted to a guy watching the game yesterday; he was enthralled and fortunately I was able to record his comments:

"Marvellous 'innit? Eighteen or nineteen grown men, all over fifty, some puffing, some panting, each coming and going, up and down the football pitch – this way and that way, come on, don't dilly dally – my old mans a dustman" – raucous humour and good natured banter abound from all involved..

Everyone having fun on a mid-week morning in Moulton. "Crikey, only three quid you say?" This is supposed to be exercise isn't it – back in my day it was jumpers for goalposts now we have a pristine all weather pitch with 'proper' uprights, white and erect, glistening in the dappled sunshine of early Spring...

The game (or was it a match?) was being eagerly contested, although no one seemed to care about the score for this was not what it was all about.

Smiling assassins pummelling the ball, bang, bang, bang, goal..!

"Marvellous 'innit?" Goalkeeper with backache by now, stooping to pick the ball out of the net again – ouch that's painful; others massaging sore thighs and aching limbs but no ice bath for this lot...brrr much too cold.

"Keep the ball down," someone shouted, "on the floor – that's it, great move – wonderful to watch – like watching Peru – sheer entertainment...

"Marvellous, 'innit...?"

# CHAPTER 6

# Derek Ellis

I played rugby all through my school and University days.

However, in my working life I landed a job with a tobacco company. Once they found out that I spoke Arabic I found myself posted to Yemen. As there was no rugby available in Yemen I was badgered into joining an expats football team - "Come on Del, you're fit you can do all the running for us" (not much has changed except I'm doing all the walking now). My social life changed drastically, and instead of downing multitudes of pints after a rugby match, I found myself chewing qat on a Thursday afternoon, (a narcotic drug that Yemeni males chew most afternoons) to be followed by playing footy on a Friday morning. (The Yemeni weekend was Thursday pm and Friday).

I'm afraid we played the Allardyce way - knock them about and hit the long ball. The average Yemeni male is approximately 5ft 5inches (think of Prince Naseem Hamed, the boxer).

We won most games from corners and free kicks with headers in the box.

The pitches were sand and stone which soon cut down on our sliding tackles, but didn't stop the odd one going through from the back to let them know you were there! (Rugby was still in the blood..!) Corner posts were often marked by a rock, and the touch line, a row of stones.

On some occasions an enterprising local lad would turn up with a bag of cement, the corner was cut out and he would walk round the pitch marking out the perimeter and penalty area. The centre circle or D on the box might get half done depending on how the cement bag was lasting.

After 5 years of playing in Yemen and 2 in Kuwait, which ended when Saddam decided to come and join the fun, I ended up in Jersey where I played for a local club for 8 years. Sporting club Francais, which was made up of Scots, Scousers and 2 local Jersey lads.

Having played rugby and football all my life I finally had to call a halt at the age of 53 due to a very necessary knee replacement operation, and I then had to become used to the fact that my competitive sporting days were over. The days of coming downstairs one at a time, sideways, like a crab, on a Sunday morning after the game were, sadly, over.

I missed my footie greatly but over the ensuing years since the operation I had finally come to terms with it until one day, when browsing a BBC website, I found an article about Walking Football.

After a bit of research, I came across the Moulton Masters webpage and got in touch with Phil Andrews who offered me a chance to try it, and even offered to lend me a pair of boots as the club kept several spares for potential new players.

To my astonishment I was hooked immediately – no drugs or any amount of alcohol could match the thrill of just being able to play football again – and me with an artificial knee and now approaching my 60th year...!

I felt like I was 18 again and suddenly had my old swagger back, and gradually the fitness came with the bonus of me losing half a stone in weight, and throughout my playing time I was enjoying swapping stories and banter with a great bunch of really welcoming blokes.

Twice a week the 35 minute drive was eagerly undertaken to get back on the pitch...

My biggest worry was that my metal knee would feel the strain too much, but this was unfounded and my whole life took on a brighter turn for the next twelve months or so...

Sadly, my remaining 'good' knee was the first to give me problems after a lifetime of abuse, and I had to limit my game time to once a week, but filled the void by refereeing games for my teammates as this was almost as much fun as playing, and meant I was still involved with the banter and bonhomie of the club.

During the Covid lockdown I had been called in for replacement knee surgery for my other knee, and having been side-lined for many months, I am now missing my football madly – especially as the others have returned to full time sessions again. I'm even looking forward to the days when I get moaned at for the standard of my refereeing – although the 'moans' were always with a smile and no malice was ever present in any of the games I witnessed.

I am now anxious just to become involved again and really looking forward to the banter and joshing.

For now, I still dream of playing again which is the incentive for me to get through the months of physio and pain barriers that I must overcome, followed by the boredom of rehab and idleness.

I'm still looking forward to seeing all the guys again and I am sure that one day "I'll be back....!"

Editor's note: We are all delighted to add that 'Del-boy' is now back playing and refereeing again...

Steve Batchelor

# CHAPTER 7

# Sandra Riley

The following is an extract from a Radio Northampton interview with Northampton Town's Women's Walking Footballer, Sandra Riley, in April 2019 and has been reproduced for this book with her permission.

Sandra trained regularly with the men at Moulton Masters and illustrates perfectly the inclusivity of the club...

I had a football at my feet as soon as I could walk....my Dad insisted. I literally kicked a football 365 days of the year, up the park and often in the garden, until it was dark. I was born in 1965, and where I lived girls found football inaccessible. Our school team did not allow girls, so my Dad took a few of us over the park with tent posts as goalposts and kit sewn by my Mum, and challenged any groups of boys that turned up. Every school holiday I would take my ball up to the local recreation ground and wait on the sidelines to be picked for a game. When I reached 16 the football stopped completely; friends moved away, and I was left with Hockey, Badminton and Swimming as my only competitive options.

I never forgot football, but it was 18 years before I ever played again in a team; it was a works 5 a side indoor set-up and I loved it. I played for a year then fell pregnant and playing football disappeared again.

Jump forward to 2018 and the BBC did an article on Walking Football, I was straight on Google to look for a club; first call I got the stock answer, 'I guess we don't have any women'. The second club I tried I hit the jackpot: they had a couple of women and I could go along. I was so excited, and that was the start of my journey. I currently attend 2 sessions a week: one on Tuesdays at the club that said yes, **Moulton Masters,** in a mixed set up (but they have sessions on Monday and Fridays as well), and Northampton Town Walking Football Club, who have helped us grow by allowing us to initially steal the top end of their pitch so that 8 women can kick a ball about. Here I have, with the help of some fantastic women, set up a women's team for 35+. We play for 2 hours on a Wednesday night, and currently have more than 30 women on our books.

Covid 19 was a real worry as we lost pitch slots and eventually pitches, but the women of this club are dedicated, and if I can find a pitch they will turn up and play! Since the last return from lockdown in 2021, we have seen an upturn in interest, with maybe 12 enquiries in March/April and most of those signing up. I have been fairly lucky with injuries - I have a touch of sciatica and usually feel it in my quads the first few games back from a rest - but nothing broken ...touch wood. The key is to warm up and cool down and plenty of stretches, but we are women, and are all guilty of a bit of a chinwag before we play and stretching sometimes gets missed. Our club is a sociable set up with players aged from 35 to 70 and we arrange teams to mix that up. Any new starters are advised it's an inclusive club, not a sports club: ladies come to sessions for all sorts of reasons with the single common factor being that we love football. Covid also took away any opportunities for tournaments really, but we did manage between lockdowns we did manage a friendly with neighbouring Bedford, thanks to Linda Thomas for organising with me.

Walking Football definitely helps you get in shape - just check your Fitbit after a session and you will easily have done your 10,000 steps, and you will have enjoyed every minute of doing them, as well as building up some chuckle muscles. Seriously it is also brilliant for a person's mental health. You can guarantee there will always be someone on WhatsApp or Messenger or at the end of a phone if you need help, and I take duty of care very seriously. I absolutely love this group of women; I always say, "Football is just a ball on the grass without a team".

Highlights so far - seeing women come with little confidence and who are now bossing the play. Reading comments in WhatsApp from one player thanking another player for helping her become better. This week one of our women was selected for the England 60+ regional squad with a chance now to represent her country and it doesn't get better than that. Congratulations to Mary Sanders. The future: well, Linda and I have just secured the first women's walking festival for Northamptonshire. It's still in the planning stages but pencilled in for June 12th, and to be hosted by Kettering Town FC. My ideal would to be to develop enough clubs within the County and borders to enable us to run a league each year. I'm sure that's not far enough and if clubs take on a 'cradle to grave policy' and embrace Walking Football under their club umbrella, as is being trialled at the moment in our club, you could start playing at 7 and stay until you are 70. My family have always known I was football mad, so this is no shock to them, and they are very supportive of me.

**Additional comment from Sam Riley, Sandra's daughter:**

As your lovely daughter (and occasional stand-in goalie) I am so very proud of you: the work you put into this is inspiring.

I knew you were football crazy for as long as I can remember and it's been an honour to play with you at a sport that is your passion. Football makes you glow with happiness and I for one am so glad to see you enjoy yourself doing something you adore. I will never tire of you spouting about football, even if I still don't understand half of what you're saying or if you're gone for hours at a time for matches.

It is always a blessing to have you home all worn out and smiling as you tell me about how it went, and the antics you guys get up to, and I can't stress enough about how proud I am, and now look at you! Doing interviews! Football is what you were born to do, the game is in your blood.

Grandad is cheering you on from the sidelines because I know in my heart of hearts that he is just as proud as me.

Steve Batchelor

# CHAPTER 8

# Simon Elliot

Simon has no claim to fame on the football pitch other than falling over whilst playing in Gary Hooper's boots during Matt Sparrow's testimonial, in front of 3,500 spectators who burst out laughing to the chant of "you fat Ba....". You can guess the rest, but he does have a claim to fame off the field as a Director of Scunthorpe United - getting promoted twice to the championship and once via the playoff final at Wembley.

However, his biggest claim to fame is spotting a young player on loan at Rushden & Diamonds from Sheffield United. Simon spotted him playing, and Scunthorpe United FC paid £100,000 for the lad, who they sold back to Sheffield United two seasons later for £2,000,000. That player has since gone on to cult status in Sheffield and respected throughout the game - he is Billy Sharp...!

Simon played for Ravensthorpe when he was in Northampton, but girls, work and golf took over when he realised that he wasn't that good on the football pitch.

Even surpassing the Billy Sharp story is Simon's unique skills as an inventor. Thomas Edison may have invented the lightbulb, Karl Benz the motorcar and Alexander Graham Bell the telephone, but it was Moulton Masters very own Simon Elliott who conceived, invented, designed and manufactured 'The Dongle'; the measuring thing, the widget, it's been called lots of things but its official patented name is the 'P.A.T.' or the 'Precision Arc Tool' - the golf ball attached to some tangled rope attached to a small paving slab that is used for the official marking out of the penalty area in all Walking Football matches held at Moulton FC – I'm sure everyone agrees that it has saved hours of measuring and countless arguments and inconsistencies with the goal area, all thanks to Simon...!

Simon involved himself a great deal in our club; other than shouting a lot, he cut the grass, organised tournaments, arranged our teams, took minutes at our committee meetings and organised our ill-fated Euro Copa trip to the Algarve, which is why there are a select few of us that have the red Moulton training tops and the black and white stripe shirts sponsored by Vans Direct. He worked hard organising everything for us only for Covid to scupper what would have been a great trip, but the miracle was he got all our money back from the organisers, even Ryan Air...!

Simon is now plying his trade up near Barnard Castle playing for Middleton Wanderers and has promised a mini tournament up North with his first love, Moulton Masters, top of the invitation list in the very near future...

# ALGARVE
## FOOTBALL TOURS

**ARE PROUD TO ANNOUNCE THE FOLLOWING
TEAMS PARTICIPATING IN**

## EUROCOPA 2020 WALKING FOOTBALL TOURNAMENT
### FROM ENGLAND

FULHAM FC                  WIMBLEDON

# EUROCOPA
**Walking Football Tournament**
ALBUFEIRA
www.algarvefootballtours.com

Poster for European Walking Football Tournament
involving Moulton Masters WFC

**Sadly postponed due to Covid-19 outbreak**

Steve Batchelor

# CHAPTER 9

# Dave Phillips

Having started work in 1972 earning the princely sum of £8 per week as an articled clerk at a firm of accountants, I eventually climbed the ladder to become Financial Director for many years until I finally hung up my calculator and retired in March 2019.

People kept asking, "What are you going to do in your retirement?" and even suggested I undertake some part time book-keeping work, to which I replied with a firm "No, thanks," as I'd had enough and now wanted a complete break from that stuff…!

My plan was to enjoy myself travelling, keeping fit, catching up with hobbies and generally spending more time at home instead of the workplace. I did plenty of homework on 'things to do in your retirement', including reading through a local publication of a fifty-plus magazine.

It was here that I first read about Walking Football at Moulton which seemed quite appealing, despite the fact that I hadn't kicked a football for over forty years, as my football career ended with the Boys Brigade…!

I decided to pluck up the courage and contacted the main man, Phil Andrews, who provided me with some basic information and was encouraging about having me join. The rest, as they say, is history...

I went along to one of the Walking Football sessions as a spectator and was introduced to some of the players. They seemed a friendly bunch who liked a bit of a laugh, and it all seemed so positive so I decided to join up.

I had to borrow some 'Sondico' boots from the club for my first game and was advised where to buy my own if I wanted to continue. To say I was a bit rusty is an understatement but at least I was made welcome and made to feel part of the team. After the game I was completely cream crackered and by the following day could hardly walk due to my aching legs. Certain muscles clearly hadn't been used for many years..!

After a while, my ability to last for an hour gradually improved and I managed to actually contribute something to the team, which was probably the most rewarding aspect. When I scored my first goal, I felt like punching the air and doing somersaults. Thankfully, I managed to restrain myself as goal celebrations may be appropriate in the Premiership, but not really the thing at Moulton Masters!

So, Walking Football at Moulton on Tuesdays and Fridays came as a real bonus in my retirement – so much so that I soon realised that this was actually the most enjoyable aspect of my non-working life (apart from spending more time with my wife, Denise, of course!). I picked up an injury at a tournament in the summer of 2019 and had to miss playing for about six weeks, which was most frustrating and quite depressing. Walking Football had already become such an important part of my life that it was hard to cope without it. Then, of course, came the 2020 lockdowns, which not only prevented me from playing my beloved football, but also curtailed most of my other planned retirement activities such as swimming and travelling. In the very last game before the first lockdown, I somehow managed to score both goals in a 2-0 victory, so at least I was able to bask in the glory of that for some time afterwards! Although I missed the football during lockdown, it was not quite as bad as being out through injury, as everyone was in the same boat and no games were taking place for anyone.

It was not only the football that I missed through lockdown, but also the camaraderie, as Moulton Masters is like one big happy family. However, the socially distanced training sessions and Zoom quizzes which were arranged, at least enabled some continuity of the social aspect.

Now back playing again through most of 2021, I'm loving every minute of it. There seem to be quite a few Dave's amongst the Masters members, so if two or three happen to play in the same team, it can be quite confusing. When someone shouts "pass it to Dave", by the time you've worked out which Dave to pass to, someone's tackled you and you've lost the ball! They've been trying to get round this by calling me 'Little Dave'. Ah well, great things come in small sizes.

Playing Walking Football for Moulton Masters is a real privilege. The pitches and facilities are first class and the members are just a great bunch of people. When the final whistle is blown on a Tuesday, I'm slightly happier than when it's blown on a Friday, the reason being that there's only 3 days to wait for the next game after Tuesday, whereas there are 4 days to wait after Friday. That is an indication of the importance of 'the beautiful game' (of the walking variety) in my life and the significant contribution it makes to my wellbeing in my twilight years.

Long may it continue.

**Editor's note:** I can see how Dave became a Financial Director by resolving such complex mathematical issues as how many days between each session.

After we returned from lockdown Dave bought his daughter along to a session to watch from the stands. He then put on a terrific performance scoring the first two goals of the game. However, his hat-trick was an embarrassing own goal as he stuck his leg out and diverted a wayward shot past his own goalie! I'm sure his daughter was very proud despite his gaffe, which we all reminded him of after the game...

# CHAPTER 10

# David Shrewsbury

Lockdown March – July 2020 stopped my 30-year-old weekly fix of indoor 6 a side football.

Other things had to take its place, like the Thursday night street clap for the NHS. This gathering enabled 75th V E Day celebrations in the street and then decided to celebrate our 50th wedding anniversary. All observing the social distance regulations.

Boris Johnson allowed a longer distance cycle ride and in June I spotted a lifelong friend in his front garden as I was passing. He advised it was time I had an e-bike and I should try Walking Football at the club in the village (Moulton). At 74 years old I said I was too young for these changes as I liked running.

We had decided that in March we would put our house 'Bryn Coed' on the market. This was a thirty-year project where we had built a house from scratch on a jungle covered plot that no one wanted, 176 miles away at Penrhyndeudraeth in North Wales. Maintaining a ¾ acre garden was becoming difficult and there was no longer "a welcome in the hillside" as Gwynedd Council were imposing 200% Council Tax on second homeowners. Tom Parry had the instructions, but lockdown prevented action.

In July the border was open, and we returned for a few days to deal with the jungle made by the good weather. Tom Parry was organising viewings, so we returned to make further progress on removing the jungle at the end of the month. This visit turned out to be the root of my tussle with a dis-functional NHS. I was using garden shears on some harder wood in carrying out my extreme gardening. On returning home on 1st August my hands swelled and the rest of my body followed in shock leaving me with a restriction in movement.

In using the self-diagnosis option on the surgery website, a doctor gave advice with a promise of physio but disappeared, never to return. In desperation I went to A&E who threw me out saying a fortnight was too long from the incident. Eventually on the 8th of September I had a phone conversation with my doctor who texted me a link for my mobile phone. With the phone propped on the windowsill he said those hands are awful, and with some pills and a referral to the Rheumatology Department at Northampton General Hospital some relief was possible.

In the meantime, mid-August, another family friend, Steve Barrs, phoned to say he was recovering from knee surgery and was playing Walking Football at Moulton, would I be interested in joining him? Thirty years previously Steve had introduced me to indoor 6 a side football at the Boys Brigade Headquarters in the Mayorhold. I needed something to combat the stiffness, aches, and pains that I was not used to, so I went along to a Monday evening match.

On arrival I was asked to stand against the wall and be shot. What a greeting? Simon Elliot was taking head and shoulders photos of members that subsequently appeared attached to the minutes of a Moulton Masters committee meeting. This has proved to be an invaluable document in recognising new teammates and the opposition. Once allocated to a game bubble the group remained the same and it was not until recent months one has been able to mix with the whole membership of 100 players.

Moulton Masters immediately gave the impression of a well-oiled machine, relying entirely on voluntary help. Everyone is informed of referees, goalkeepers and first aid equipment for a game.

There are, of course, new rules to understand including wearing the correct boots for a 4G pitch. Phil Andrews was on inspection at the gate and had me lifting my hooves. It was like being at the farriers. That desire to run has been knocked out of me but some referees obviously do not see that I am moving with my heels down and rely on "you're too quick". Our age means a reoccurrence of the effects of old abuse and the need to rest and repair. Nonetheless this is a glowing tribute to the caring organisers who wish us all a good game.

Twelve months has passed, and I have learnt a lot from those that have played to a higher standard in the original game, both phraseology and technique. Now, at 75 years old I am glad I found a new interest in Walking Football, and yes on long rides I now use an e-bike. A tribute then to the advice of old friends.

# CHAPTER 11

# Stuart Fraser

At the very young age of five I ended up in hospital for over a year because of a diseased call Perthes. It's treated in a completely different way these days but when I was a youngster it was dealt with by a major operation and a long stay in hospital, and a long recovery period. My mum was told I'd be in a wheelchair by the time I reached my 20's, and I was wearing callipers and specially made shoes to help me walk again. I used to play football with these structures wrapped around my leg and was often first picked to play because nobody wanted to tackle me in case they got hurt.

Needless to say, I never ended up in a wheelchair - in fact, quite the reverse. I became very competitive, although I do still walk with a limp to this day.

I became one of the fastest runners in the school of 1,500 pupils and entered many different sports, including football. I didn't really get into football until my mid 20's and played for the fire brigade - no skill, just pure fitness, all attack, and everyone defends.

I also played regular games against CID Bedford but my claim to fame was running 3 eleven-a-side teams at a company called Unipath, in Bedford, where we used to play local teams or each other, and entered the odd tourney with little effect.

I only ever got the one trophy for player of the year, and I still have it today. I like to attack but play better as a defender, so they used to say, but since I got kicked out of the fire brigade through injury I found myself unable to play anymore. I've had over 14 knee operations on my right knee including 3 knee replacements, and again a knee replacement in my left knee; I was never going to play football again, or so I thought.

I saw an advert, on a notice board for Walking Football, so called the number and spoke to Phil, who invited me to come and look.

I guess this is the bit you really want. I never thought I'd play any sort of sport again involving the use of my legs. In my first game of Walking Football, I could only kick the ball a matter of a few yards and walking was more of a slow march, but I did really enjoy being outside and playing the game.

I continued to come to the games and slowly I began to improve, not only in the game, but also in meeting new friends. Getting out and about has been in a decline for many so keeping up with mates was hard. I hadn't realised how much I had lost until I started making new friends at MM. I'm not sure how long I can keep playing for, but yes, it has been great so far and a great lift to one's mental health.

**Editor's note:** Stuart is one of those gems in a group who turns a team into a club. By that I mean that he has particular skills that help improve 'our lot'.

Being unofficial club photographer at multiple events, producing laser etched sizes on all club spare boots, making hand carved gifts for players departing, designing tournament pitch layouts with dedicated pitch numbers and producing a generator to power the laptop for real time tournament scoring.

Most importantly, he also regularly gives this editor a lift to training sessions!

# CHAPTER 12

# Richard Jobling

My story of getting back to playing football with Moulton Masters is the final part of my rejuvenation for the love of the beautiful game. When I was a young man living in Northolt in West London, in my teenage years and up to my mid 20's, life revolved around football, rock music, drinking and occasionally, women. Saturdays were taken up with Queens Park Rangers, down the pub and off to a Nightclub. Sunday mornings, aged 21 from 1984 to 1988, I was playing for a team in the North Hillingdon District league. We were a decent team; I played Centre Half and I scored the winner in the 1988 North Hillingdon League Cup Semi-final. So off we went to the final, but I got a bad knee injury playing in a league game, got clobbered in revenge for a previous encounter the week before the final and could not play. Our team went on to win the final. I was really pissed off about this and decided to stop playing the following season; anyway I was due to get married a few months later and my girlfriend, now wife, was relieved that I stopped playing as invariably I got an injury towards the end of a season, which usually involved a trip to Northwick Park Hospital for an afternoon at A&E. I had a bit of a reputation for getting stuck in and usually came off worse.

We bought a house in Northampton, got married and moved there in April 1989. I worked in London and commuted, which I did until 2017, but my biggest regret on the playing football front, was that when I was 26 I didn't go along to start playing again at a local club in Northampton. Kids came along and priorities changed, etc. I always followed QPR, but the real rejuvenation was being invited along by my mate, Mel to go to the 2014 Play Off Final against Derby. Oh my God! It all came flooding back - the love for the game, seeing some old QPR mates I hadn't seen for years. I was hooked and by the next season I had a season ticket and off I went then to QPR each home game, meeting up with my best mate, Rich, and after the game at our usual pub on the Shepherds Bush Road, to talk football and the world. We have known each other now for well over 40 years.

Well the final bit of the rejuvenation was joining Moulton Masters in September 2019. I had taken early retirement about a year earlier and at 56 was looking to fill time during the week and keep fit, when up on Facebook popped an FA advert for Walking Football. I looked through the Northants FA affiliated clubs and picked Moulton Masters. I emailed Phil Andrews who came back very quickly and said come along to the next session; he also said that there were a few other QPR guys at the club, one being Ron Marzetti. Getting to know Ron was a great help in settling within the club. We were also bonded by our love of QPR and within a few weeks of joining I was going down to mid-week QPR games with him, although we broke down once at Savoy Circus on the A40 Western Avenue and I still remember him crying out, "the clutch has gone Rich, we're going to break down," and we did too. I limped off with my dodgy left knee (injured that week) to Loftus Road to watch our usual FA Cup humiliation, and Ron stayed valiantly with the car until later in the evening to wait for the RAC.

The old West London connection (he comes from Hayes, next door to Northolt), led Dave Hetherington, after a few weeks, naming us the West London mafia, and obviously Ron, with his Italian surname, is now known as the Godfather. Anyway, on that first Tuesday game, Phil asked what position I play, and I said striker - the rest is history, I scored the winner in a 2-1 victory. I was hooked straight away, went off and bought a new pair of football boots and now just love the get together each week. It has been good to make new friends, having a coffee after the game and a chat with the guys, and all the banter that goes with it.

John Austin thinks I have an Excel spreadsheet to record all my goals and assists (not as many as Steve B). Actually I do have an Access database, alongside my gigs attended and CD collection databases.

**Editor's note:** With Steve B already here, and Ron Marzetti joining, I wanted to limit the amount of QPR fans at our club but had to relent when a fourth and then a fifth R's supporter joined – where have they all been hiding?

# CHAPTER 13

# Les Goodridge

Watching and playing football has always been a big part of my life. I've supported Northampton Town all my life, having lived near to the old county ground.

I never played for any local club and only really played for fun; playing for the Bat & Wickets (local pub) was the peak of my career. Many years ago I started to play regularly with a youth group but eventually gave up as it became very competitive, and extremely physical. I retired from work in 2016 and saw the Barclay card advert for Walking Football, which wasn't very inspiring, but thought I'd give it a go. I found a group who were playing at Malcolm Arnold school.

That was the turning point, and the Walking Football bug took hold. It has given me a chance to play a sport that I love, and playing two to three times a week has kept me fit and healthy. As a youngster I was always in goal or a striker, and I have been able to improve my goalkeeping skills. Who would have thought that at 63 I would still be playing and getting enjoyment from making saves?

Playing in tournaments has been another challenge; it's funny how the competitive edge is still there, even though you are only playing for fun! And to cap it all I won my first football medal at 61 when Moulton Masters were runners up in the inaugural Northamptonshire County Cup.

I've now started to play on the pitch more and this is certainly a challenge to my fitness, let alone my football skills.

Since taking up Walking Football I have met some great people, made some new friends and become reacquainted with some old friends, and it has helped with both my physical and my mental health.

# CHAPTER 14

# Andy Stevenson

**Walking Football & Type 2 Diabetes, the journey so far**

I confess to not being, what I consider, a real diabetic. That title, in my opinion, is reserved for those brave souls who inject insulin and constantly monitor their blood sugar levels throughout the day. Perhaps that is some of you? Currently I fly the flag for Type 2 but have been told in no uncertain terms that the needle awaits if I do not get my blood sugar levels under proper control. Having been diagnosed a few years ago following daily periods of tiredness/lethargy at work (School teacher for 36 years) I was given the option to control or even possibly reverse this degenerative condition using 'diet and exercise'. Subsequent check-ups concluded however that this was not enough (or perhaps I was not taking it seriously) and now I have been prescribed a range of strange sounding medications in order to keep my blood sugar under stricter control.

Nearly three years ago, under instruction, I started to play Walking football at Redwell, Wellingborough, in an effort to lose weight and generally improve cardio-vascular function. The opportunity to play the beautiful game once again was grabbed with both hands after an interval of several years from when I had played Veterans at Corby in such famed company as Dave Trussler and Ron Marzeti. Prior to that I played football for the County at junior school but when I moved up to secondary at 11 years of age the head of P.E. insisted that I play Rugby because I was very tall for my age and was good in the line outs!

The gym never really interested me and being a keen football supporter (going to games at Cambridge, Luton and England, putting money through the turnstiles etc) playing was always a close second, although now, as time runs out, I would rather play than watch.

So, as my walking football journey continued I began to lose weight, feel more awake and generally feel of better mental health. During the lockdowns when the walking football was not available my weight started to creep back on again, so I knew that playing was having a positive effect. I was then introduced to Moulton Masters and the opportunity to play more which is proving to be, dare I say, life changing.

I soon began to overthink, as one does perhaps when things are going well. During some games I began to feel cold/tired and worried about having some kind of hypo incident where the exercise had reduced blood sugar to such a level that I might go dizzy or worse. I remember Gary Mabbutt the Spurs midfielder was one of the first top players to 'come out' with this condition. It worried me about when to take my meds as I did not want a blood sugar clearance before or during a game and as the meds must be taken with food and I didn't want to feel bloated either. Pre match Energy drinks were a definite no as these contained like a whole day's sugar intake and would cause a massive spike. Sugar free Red Bull was tried and while the caffeine helped me to concentrate more during the game (or did it, maybe I should have tried a placebo?) but it also stopped me sleeping, especially Monday nights after games when I often drove home buzzing F1 style and even more so when Phil had put me in a team that actually won!

Weight loss also became a concern when it should have made me happy!

My BMI was going down gradually (that's good) but my body muscle mass was decreasing (that's bad). It seemed that while I was losing body fat I was also experiencing muscle wastage as a side effect which on investigation was it caused by my daily cocktail of diabetic medication, or perhaps just ageing? My arms and legs were getting very thin (that's why I always wear tracksuit bottoms) but tummy fat decrease remains much less noticeable, I was becoming a fat Peter Crouch.

In the colder months, with a decreased layer of insulation,

I was wearing a full set of Thermal gear under my black or white kit in an effort to keep warm. Just "wandering around the pitch" (quote from Pat Curtis on my playing style) was not generating enough heat. My weight loss was becoming far too complicated. What was worrying me were the occasional malfunction in moments of passion!

More tablets were prescribed and corrected and even improved my shots on target tremendously.

Eyesight is also a diabetic concern and I have free eye tests annually at Specsavers, which look for irregularities in the retina. I have good results on this but seem to have an above average number of 'floaters' and 'spidery webs' in my visual field which sometimes makes me see a swarm of flies rushing toward me and can create problems whilst reading. I put any stray shots or passes on the pitch down to this and there are several of both in most games.

We play the game with our feet and one of the big worries for diabetics is nerve damage by high blood sugar levels to these extremities and the risk of possible eventual amputation. I still get considerable stabbing pains nightly in my feet and toes, but these nasties have decreased thankfully and I put this down to the stimulation offered by the walking in studded boots (I'm a Sondico man) and ball contact afforded during a game, it has to be beneficial.

Getting my feet trodden on regularly (especially by Rob Baston) is actually reassuring as I can feel the pain, so I know the nerves are working. I also look after my feet and inspect and moisturise them most nights, perhaps to the point of obsession but not perversity.

To conclude, my diabetes and walking football have become entwined, and each has a massive respect for the other. I have lost around 18 pounds in the last year, and this slowly continues which must have massive long term benefit. My G.P. is very happy and all the complicated blood sugar numbers are looking handsome. If I had to stop playing, I am sure that my future would be insulin injection which although manageable would feel like a crushing defeat to me.

# CHAPTER 15

# Mark Simpson

**Game Changer**

Retirement brought me an opportunity to restore some fitness. Leading the charge was a daily cycling trip around Pitsford Reservoir with the object of improving my circuit times. I supplemented this with longer trips accompanied by Tony Burwood. It was on one of these trips that he mentioned a new sport he was trying called 'Walking Football (WF)'. It was a brief discussion and I thought nothing more about it until a few weeks later, when another friend and neighbour, 'Deano' Barron, asked me if I fancied checking out Walking Football as he was going to give it a try. Aha, I thought, I've heard about this and wasn't too enthused at the time, but thought I might as well look into it after all.

One Autumn Monday evening back in 2019 - don't ask me which month, as I can't remember - Deano and I strolled into a noisy changing room - well it was until we arrived. Arranged on the benches were a bunch of elderly blokes in a variety of clothing that included recognised kit plus a mix of hats, jumpers, gloves, leggings and bandages. The stares and accompanying silence were broken by an official looking bloke holding a clipboard who asked us who we were.

So, we told him our names - here for the football we said. He responded with, "I'm Phil, the club chairman. What boots have you got?" Trainers we said. "Can't wear those - not allowed" he responded, but graciously followed up with, "we have spare pairs you can borrow - make sure you hand them back. Session fees are £4.00 for those working, £3.00 for those that aren't. We have to pay for the lights on a Monday, Tuesday and Friday. Daytimes are £3.00 and £2.00. First session is free to see if you like it".

After explaining we had never played the sport before and receiving a brief overview we kitted up and headed out to the pitch. Our first impressions must have been similar to those players who step onto the hallowed Wembley turf for the first time.

What a superb facility, virtually brand new latest technology surface, floodlighting, with a clubhouse and bar as well. Surprise, surprise, on our pitch was Tony Burwood. So this was the place he had been telling me about. After warm up exercises we were honoured by having Phil as the referee, but I must admit that I was having early doubts about the sport when, after being accused of fouling an opposition player and politely querying if his backing in was an offence, I not only gave a free kick away but was also sin binned for two minutes for dissent - really?

My only consolation was that teammates Dean Baron and Tony Burwood also suffered similar fates at various stages in the game. On the journey home we discussed our experiences. 'Enjoyed it' was the consensus but the ref seemed a real strict type (or words to that effect). The following three days were agony as muscles I had not used in anger for years made their distress known in the form of stiffness, aches and pains, and a walk John Wayne would have been proud of. Originally starting in goal, an injury to my shoulder whilst unsuccessfully trying to dive to stop a penalty shot meant I gave up that position and this reminded me that I carried far more weight and didn't bounce like I did in my younger days.

So, that was our introduction to the world of Walking Football. It's not just a sport and form of exercise but has the benefit of widening your social circles, which is helpful following retirement. It has a positive effect of improving your physical and mental well-being. Once the initial barriers of joining an established membership are broken down, the characters who form this illustrious group are revealed. Players originated from various parts of the country, evidenced by the replica football kit they wear, their accents and suitably appropriate nicknames (it was months before I knew 'Scouse' was really called Terry).

The club is an active hotbed of fan groups, led by the Northampton Town 'crew' and tales abound of what was, is and hopefully will be. Names of the old Cobblers professional and amateur players - who most of us non-locals have never heard of - are spoken of in awe and reverence. 'Little' Ron (not to be confused with Big Ron), Richard and Stevie Batch are very enthusiastic QPR fans and Walking Football forwards with an insatiable hunger for scoring goals and talking extensively about both topics after a game.

The diverse spread of personalities at the club ranges from the quiet and reserved to the opposite end of the spectrum.

An example of this is our subscription collection team. They do a great job at every session, booking in the players, collecting payments and directing them to their respective pitches and teams.

'Jaymo' is the soul of discretion, and merely raises an eyebrow or gives the occasional quietly worded response - no expletives - when pulled up for a rare game infringement, simply observing that it was a 'rather excessive' reaction by the ref. His counterpart, Dave H, relishes every opportunity to make good-natured jibes at players, officials and the world in general. Dave has an opinion for every situation and every situation needs his opinion, backed up by a parade ground delivery.

In the early days of the club, when the player base was smaller, match team selection was straightforward. The organiser walked around the pitch handing out a coloured bib and giving each player a number. The first time I experienced this system, Dave H approached me and said 'you are a number two'. At first I felt aggrieved at this perceived insult and was preparing a suitable retort, until I heard him repeat it to several other players and the penny dropped.

Phil, the chairman, has been dedicated to expanding the club from its roots of 5 men and a dog (it's said the dog was the outstanding player) and raising its profile within the sport and wider community. He is exactly the type of individual that Moulton Masters needs to make the club a success and it wouldn't be at its 100+ membership level today without him. He has embraced social media for communication but as the uptake of this varies across the membership, pen to paper and even talking to people are approaches that are still employed. His communications are legendary for their length and attention to detail but do demand a robust constitution to get through them all.

On the pitch he moves remarkably quickly for someone who says he has so many injuries and ailments with more metalwork inside him than British Steel, so sometimes it's difficult to believe him. He has had his share of bad luck whilst at the club. A pre-season trip to watch The Cobblers in Spain resulted in him injuring his back and then due to laying on the hotel floor for relief he also caught a chill. He returned home nearly completely incapacitated and this was his temporary introduction to the Zimmer frame. Then there was the time when an errant shot from another pitch hit him on the back of the head and he suffered mild concussion resulting in a hospital visit.

Every player contributes to the success of the club. Special thanks go to those involved in match organisation and the club officials. The diverse and good natured atmosphere combined with the support given to members who are experiencing problems and challenges in their everyday lives is a much appreciated benefit.

In addition to 'fit' players, there is always an active group of those recovering from illness and injury who turn up to watch, provide satirical feedback and join the socialising around the games.

Despite their maturing years, players are not dissuaded from playing under adverse and extreme weather conditions. Memories abound of hot summer days when only mad dogs and Moulton Masters Walking Football players go out in the midday sun, through to winter evenings when the downpour is being blown horizontally across a pitch occupied by a soggy bunch of players doing their best to emulate sailors in a storm. They present a humorous picture, but there is a serious side as these conditions can lead to heat exhaustion and hypothermia. Also, it has become evident over time that symptoms experienced when playing are sometimes as a result of underlying conditions that need professional medical attention and not solely down to participating.

The club has evolved practices and procedures along with first aid training to mitigate the effects of the weather conditions and in-game player injuries. The WF rules are designed to minimise contact and mitigate associated injuries but pulled muscles and the resurgence of old problems are commonplace. For the most part the club has a laid back, friendly atmosphere but the vagaries of human nature surface when the matches get underway and the old competitive streak kicks in.

For some this is a minor affliction, but for others there is a noticeable shift in temperament. The looks of disappointment, frustration and angst bubble to the surface when the game, or a player's contribution, is not going in the right direction: missed goal scoring opportunities, poor passing, bad positional play, teammates' contribution, perceived injustice in a ref's decision and worst of all, losing. Thankfully back at the clubhouse adrenalin levels drop, and the results are dissected with a returning sense of humour. The merits of skills such as doing a 'Littlemore' (speculative back heel), 'Stevie Batch' (spin and shoot) and 'Lionel' (too close? He was backing in) 'Jim Led' (I never run), 'Derek Krajewski' (They will never score past me from that angle) are critiqued.

Then there is the refereeing role which is undertaken by a few individuals who also play at the club. Overall, players may not always agree with the ref's decisions, but they value the job they do. This is a Marmite responsibility which appeals to a limited audience, but which is a great opportunity for players to get a view from the 'Dark Side'. It helps to be relatively thick skinned and have good communication skills, but it can still be pretty onerous at times. Despite the supposed more gentle nature of the game most players comment on decisions in the heat of the moment, which usually comprise a one-off reaction and the game moves on. Of course, there are times when the discussion becomes protracted and other actions have to be taken. Offering to hand over the refereeing responsibilities to the individual is an effective solution, or in the worst cases, a two-minute sin bin will have the desired effect. As in the standard game the perspective and interpretation of a player and ref usually differ, this also applies between players on opposite teams. Walking Football introduces more constraints, including ball height from the ground, no running, limited contact and areas at each end restricted to the goalkeeper. All of these increase the difficulty of the ref's job and more of the associated discussions that result from interpretation of the law or situation. Added to this are the problems with each individual's faculties - especially listening - despite repeated whistle blows and shouting, getting players attention is a challenge. Pre-match briefings are sometimes difficult due to the background conversations persistently carrying on. Water breaks can be like herding cats when trying to get players back to restart, as they are having chinwags with team-mates, or the 'crowd,' and their focus is elsewhere.

The club has had successes with individuals trialling for England and Dave Poole being selected in goal. Dave, being a very modest individual, tends to keep this low key but demonstrated a steely resolve to represent his country despite an ongoing illness and a number of game injuries. He is renowned for his extensive historic knowledge of the amateur game in Northampton and associated players. He also tends to be one of the later arrivals on pitch especially when applying extensive strapping for goal keeping duties.

Thoughts go out to those players who are no longer at the club because of outside commitments, game-ending injuries and losing the fight against illness. To name but two: Johnny, who played a few games at the club and in the dying moments of his last game scored a memorable goal only to fall awkwardly and dislocate his knee, and Billy Horne who eventually lost his battle with illness but throughout maintained a quiet determination to play as much as he could. A dignified individual who always apologised for only being able to play part of a match during this time, but the enjoyment it gave him was also uplifting to others who felt privileged to be on the same pitch, and to share those special moments.

# CHAPTER 16

# Steve Barrs

My love for the game started back in 1976 at the late age of 11 when I watched Man U lose 1-0 to Southampton in the FA Cup final. I remember I was very excited as my parents had just bought our first colour TV.

Until then I hadn't shown much interest in football and I blame my father for that as he was cricket mad and hated football but I have to thank my dad for his keenness for me to join the 6th Boys Brigade, Kingsley, Northampton.

He spent his whole youth there and became the solo drummer in the marching band and I'm proud to say that I kept up the family tradition and followed in his footsteps leading the band also. It was at the BB that football for me really kicked off (excuse the pun), I played in goal and we regularly won the league. The big game though was always on Boxing Day where the BB 'Old Boy's' would play our team and that tradition has been going on for 75 years and for the last few years I've overseen chasing the old boys to get a team together to take on the lads and I'm proud to say I've now played on Boxing Day 42 times!

I left school in 1981 and worked a summer season at a holiday camp on Hayling Island and the following summer I found myself on the Isle of Wight as a Greencoat at Warners doing 4 shows a week and was also in charge of the 10 to 15 year old children's club.It was here that we used to play a staff challenge match every week and a West Ham scout saw my performance in goal and said he was impressed and would arrange a trial with Northampton Town (Cobblers) for when I returned.True to his word there was the letter when I returned in September inviting me for a trial. I was 18 by this point and was very nervous when I arrived at the old County ground. It wasn't helped when I found myself training with all the 16-year-old Prima Donnas who thought they'd already made it and they didn't make me feel welcome in the slightest.Fortunately, the session went very well, and I seemed to stop everything and didn't concede a single goal. Afterwards the coach pulled me to one side and said he was impressed and invited me to go back the following week. Sadly, I didn't as I wasn't comfortable with the other players, and it was probably the worst decision of my life and I'm sure if my father had been a football fan, he would have insisted I get my arse back up there.About this time I was invited to get back into my other passion which was marching bands. I initially helped the drum section of a local band, but this soon led onto becoming the bandmaster and over a ten- year period we won a few National competitions.

There used to be a saying, "it's better to do an easy routine well than to do a difficult one badly" I never agreed with that and always felt it was better to do a difficult routine well. I guess that's why we were so successful.Between 1982 & 1992 I was also playing Sunday morning football in goal for the likes of St Andrews, Queens Park, SPA, The Pioneer and The Rose & Claret, but like any goalkeeper I was a frustrated striker and from the age of 28 I started playing up front and scored 26 in my first season for the Pioneer pub and 28 in my second. I then defected to the Rose and Claret and scored 4 on my debut.

After that the goals started to dry up as my knee started to deteriorate.

At the age of 37 I broke my ankle in pre-season training and spent 8 days in hospital before they could operate where I had a plate and screws fitted.

I was then asked to start and manage a new team at the Pioneer pub, so I put a team together from scratch and I'm pleased to say we won the league in our very first season.

I never played myself as we always had enough subs but I do remember one game when we only had two subs so I named myself as the third and with ten minutes to go and 17-0 up with my midfielder just scoring his 4th I subbed him and went on and scored two! Sadly, they were to be my last competitive goals. I continued to play 5 a side twice a week but eventually at the age of 42 my knee had deteriorated to a point that I could play no more, I was devastated! The game that I loved had a been taken away from me and I found that very difficult to accept and deal with. In fact, it only got worse over the following years, I've lost count how many times I'd dream that I was playing again with no pain only to wake to up in bed and feeling really low again. Then about three years ago a good friend of mine, Jim Ledington, suggested I tried walking football, but I was sceptical as I thought it would be rubbish, but I eventually went along and was blown away. Although my knee blew up and I couldn't walk again for a week I was buzzing. I also met someone with two knee replacements, and he was playing!!!

Unbeknown to him he became my inspiration to get back. I had my new knee in January 2020 and was chomping at the bit to test it.

Since then I haven't looked back, and it's been brilliant!!! Everyone has made me welcome at Moulton Masters and it's great to take part in the typical football banter on the pitch again that I'd also missed dearly. If you're missing playing football and thinking walking football is not for you, don't knock it till you've tried it.

I can assure you you'll be blown away, it's the best thing since sliced bread! Without doubt Walking Football has been my salvation.

# CHAPTER 17

# Martin Wade

As a child, football was my first love, playing for the Cubs and Scouts teams managed by my dad. Football has a way of bringing out so many emotions. Over the years I've missed penalties in finals, scored penalties in finals, won leagues, faced relegation, met some of the nicest lads and at times gained a few on-field enemies. I played for the Northampton Town Boys, numerous Town League teams, school teams and even played Semi-professional for Blisworth Town (but being a Forest fan, I only joined them as the Forest Scout would pop in to watch the odd game) - alas that was really the height of my football dream.

My memories of playing were the pungent smell of embrocation filling the air in the changing rooms, the after game pub grub and the end of season piss ups, usually on FA Cup Final day. Football, to me, was always a happy way of life. With dodgy knees, a weak ankle and the dreaded 'Clubman of the Year' award, it was finally time to try Vet's Football. Vet's Football was supposed to be an excuse to rekindle my youth, but unfortunately I soon found that the constant injuries and the sight of 22 men trying to be 18 again was not for me.

So, for a while I resorted to watching local football on a Saturday, then garden centre visits and a roast on a Sunday. That was the stage I'd got to when I heard about Walking Football, and I joined a bunch of ageing men with a love for football having a kick about during days off.

It was a difficult time for me as I'd not long lost my job and was at a pretty low place, mentally. Like all men, I chose to keep it to myself. I found that Walking Football helped to put things to the back of my mind. With the help of family, friends and a new job, my depression improved.

Walking Football had made the glorious game my first love again. With 3 sessions a week it meant I was able to juggle football with work life and home life. I've always been quite a competitive person (probably having 3 brothers helps) and our club caters for all types of players, including some tournament wins for us.

When I was a kid I used to look at the older generation and think, 'God, I really don't want to end up like these old folk?' But society these days has changed so much. At 53, I'm at the beginning of my Walking Football journey and with players at our club in their 70's I know I have many years of football to come. That hour on the pitch helps to block out the stresses and tribulations of everyday life.

Once again, I am that 8 year old kid, still LIVING THE DREAM

# CHAPTER 18

# Martin Littlemore

Linda died in October 2013 and I had a mental breakdown.

Depression set in, and for the next two years I more lor less degenerated and began drinking too much alcohol, eating too much junk food and meeting only with people from my immediate family.

My family said I needed help and through my MacMillan nurse I undertook bereavement counselling. I was also told by my doctor that I was overweight and needed to take more exercise, so I joined a local gym. Although I started going regularly and began losing weight, I was not enjoying the experience and found it hard to mix with other people as I was conscious of how ridiculous I must look as a pensioner in lycra, compared to the other gym users. However, I persevered and was feeling a little better mentally, so started to attend Northampton Town football matches again, both home and away.

Then in 2016 Barclays Bank started advertising Walking Football on TV, and being a 'Cobblers' supporter most of my life, and having played a bit in my youth, my son and daughter both said I should 'give it a go,' saying I would enjoy it much more than the gym.

That summer I kept seeing the advert and when the new football season began I looked to see where I might be able to play. At first I had no luck, but in October I was in 'Carr's Bar' at Northampton FC and recognised Phil Andrews who I knew by sight as he was also a dedicated Cobblers fan. I told him I had heard he had started a Walking Football group and could I please attend to see what it was like? He invited me to join a session at Malcolm Arnold Academy on any Monday evening, and on 7th November 2016 I joined his group. The first few session were a bit of a shambles as we were still a fledgling club with a mixed group of players, and had various interpretations of the rules, but I did find the experience immensely enjoyable.

By December we had a problem with the pitch at Malcolm Arnold as the surface was too icy and therefore too dangerous to play but Phil managed to arrange to play on the all-weather pitch at Moulton School, and we then developed a routine for going for a pint at The Telegraph after the game. I soon began to get to know the other players better and found myself once again being able to 'have a laugh,' and knew this was something I had been missing in life for some time.

By March 2017 Phil had also started to run a Friday morning session at Beckets Park and although we only had about 5 regulars we used to 'rope in' passers-by, including one day, a Chinese tourist who was clearly a better footballer than any of us and scored 7 goals in a single session!

As well as the Monday night 'proper' matches we were now playing regularly mid-week at various locations and were trying to attract passers-by to join in and 'give it a go'.

Amongst the locations we played were Abington Park, The Pastures near Kingsthorpe, Wootton Community Centre (we got hold of via the groundsman marking pitches and cutting grass), Far Cotton Rec, Parklands, Hardingstone Rec, Eastfield Park, Denton Park, West Hunsbury Country Park, The Racecourse, Dallington Park, Upton County Park, Pitsford, and at most of these venues we would all retire to a local pub afterwards for a well-earned pint.

Parklands became my regular daytime Walking Football venue where we played on a small pitch marked out for under 7's teams, and was therefore just the right size for us until it also became too muddy, so we then played indoors at

Danes Camp Leisure Centre.

In January 2018 Benham Sports Club advertised Walking Football on Tuesday but at the first session I was the only person to turn up! Having spoken with Phil we managed to get 5 of us together for the following week and soon I was playing 3 times a week: Monday evenings, and Tuesday and Friday mornings. Northampton News even sent a reporter to film and interview us as the development of Walking Football was starting to spread far and wide.

By the summer of 2018 we were having trouble with availability of bookings for Benham & Danes Camp and Phil was actively looking for a more permanent venue. Meanwhile we found ourselves back at Parklands hoping the weather would be kind.

In May 2018 we entered our first tournament to be played on the hallowed turf at Sixfields Stadium. We managed to finish as runners up in our group, and actually beat the eventual tournament winners, so were pretty pleased with ourselves.

Whilst attending Cobblers matches I found out the guy sitting next to me was a coach to a kids team at Moulton FC; his wife was club secretary and he told me of the new 3G pitch that was being installed. I explained our problem with finding daytime venues with a suitable surface and he put us in touch with the hierarchy at Moulton: Dave Conway and Pete Knight. Phil and I went to look at the pitches, then we went with Les Goodridge to talk about the possibility of playing regular Walking Football on their pitch. They readily agreed so long as we adopted the Moulton name and became synonymous with their club, to which we also agreed, and Moulton Walking Football Club was born. The first session was held on Monday 3rd September 2018, then further matches followed on the Tuesday and Friday mornings and finally we knew we had found our new home.

Phil managed to get BBC Northampton interested in Walking Football, and we were again interviewed about the development of the game and our unique club. We had also started playing other teams, and I remember a match which we lost 2-1 to Harborough but still enjoyed the buffet and beer.

As our games were expanding and more members were joining, we needed to control the games better, so Phil and a bunch of us attended a Walking Football refereeing course at Beckets School, and I occasionally began to referee games instead of playing every session

In February 2019 our 'all weather' pitch was covered in 2 inches of snow and football had to be cancelled for the first time – fortunately this was a rare occurrence

In April 2019 I took my grandson, Benjamin, aged 13, along and he played in goal in some of our matches and, although I was a bit worried about him, he played well and earned plaudits from many of the other players. This was a very special moment for me as how many footballers can say they have played in the same team as their grandson...!

We entered a Walking Football Tournament at Bedford FC for the age group 65+, and won our group with 2 wins and 2 draws before being eliminated. Not long after this we tried to start a Thursday night session to include Ladies games as we were also gaining female players. However, this was not as successful as we had hoped and eventually our 'girls' moved their base to form Northampton Ladies WFC.

In May 2019 I organised a 'race evening' for the club which was very well received with over 60 people turning up and raising quite a bit of cash for the club. The following month we hosted our first Walking Football Tournament which also went very well.

After considering various names for our club over several months we eventually settled on Moulton Masters in August 2019, as this seemed the most appropriate, especially as earlier suggestions had included Moulton 'Walking with Dinosaurs' or Moulton Very Old Boys!

On 4th October 2019 we held an over 65's Tournament to raise money for the Justin Edinburgh Trust and our first team managed to triumph as Tournament winners.

Then on 24th of this month Phil and I and a few others went along to Daventry Leisure Centre to receive the Community Sports Activity of the Year award. The following month we also went along to the Northamptonshire Sports awards at the Park Inn, and although we didn't win, we were honoured to finish in the top four

Unfortunately, 2019 was not a very good year for me and I refereed more than played, as I was constantly in pain. My Doctor was concerned that a bout of cancer for which I had been successfully treated might be returning and pretty soon the bouts of depression started to set in again.

I was prescribed steroids which made me gain weight and even though no cancer had been detected I was still constantly in pain.

By March 2020 the developments of the Covid epidemic had forced the whole Country to go into lockdown and all football had to stop. We could shop only for essential items with no mixing with people from other households, and at this stage few people realised just how serious this was.

July saw the lifting of some regulations and we were able to start Walking Football again under strict conditions, and with the changing rooms closed we all had to arrive in our kit and put our boots on in the car park.

In October 2020 Moulton Masters suffered its first serious injury when Greg Pamment snapped his Achilles and one of our players, Andy Clarke, donated a trophy to be called the 'Fighting Fit Award' to encourage him in his recovery.

November 2020 saw another lockdown in order to preserve Christmas and when this was lifted, we were able to play again, but I was still being plagued by injuries and when I fell over in one particular match I found myself covered in bruises and again began to feel very low.

My depression continued into the New Year and didn't really improve until March when we were finally able to play football again properly. My Doctor had prescribed a chemotherapy drug and said that I might have to cut down on playing, but should continue to referee and attend as a spectator as often as possible, as this was clearly good for my well-being. My grandson, Benjamin, was able to join in and play in goal again during the school holidays and this always gives me a lift.

By mid-2020 the club had formed an inaugural formal committee which I was invited to join. Amongst the many innovations, we requested all players to purchase 2 sets of bibs which we had ordered, so that we could organise our internal games better - 1 black & 1 white, and we could now easily distinguish who was playing in which team, irrespective of whether they were wearing

Northampton Town or Real Madrid kit. This idea had 100% take-up and was appreciated by all.

Myself and another player, Lionel, were responsible for club registrations and we also introduced emergency first aid training into our activities with special attention for use of the defibrillator which was held in the clubhouse. This was also very well attended.

Unfortunately, one of our newer players, Johnny Moore, badly dislocated his knee in a fall and we had to wait almost 3 hours for the ambulance to arrive.

We had learned from our first-aid training that we shouldn't move the person in this position so we could only try to keep him warm and wait.

Johnny was in hospital for some time and in plaster, so is not expected back for a while, but has already messaged the club to thank us for our support and has promised to return one day.

Not that long ago we struggled to get 10 players to a session: now we regularly have 40+ and have actually reached the milestone of 100 players affiliated to our Walking Football group.

Although playing is still a struggle, I still do so as often as possible and if not playing I always volunteer to referee or help out as much as I can. I've even found a source for club training kit that I am able to sell to our players to help with club funds and feel this club has now become an integral part of my life.

# CHAPTER 19

# Pete McCrone - Football boots

In days of yore, what boots you wore,
Showed just how good you were,
Mostly black, a little white, more stripes,
More skill - it would infer;
Now we're all like 'Fancy Dans'
With colours shining brightly,
Despite all this, it would appear
We're just not quite so sprightly.
Never mind I say, there is no shame,
We shall not give up, not ever,
Even though our poor old knees,
are feeling none too clever.
With happy hearts, we'll walk our game,
And chase our favourite sphere,
We might be slow, but we should know,
As our laughter rings loud and clear.
**Pete McCrone – unsung hero**

**ON AIR**

On Tuesday 14th September, the BBC visited Rushden's Harborough Fields Surgery to discuss the vaccination program and AFC R&D WF stalwart Pete McCrone was invited along to give his views on volunteering. Speaking on BBC Radio Northampton, Pete was able to give a valuable insight into the work being done by our volunteers, and got across just how helpful it had been for our Walking Footballers to keep in touch during the difficult first days of lockdown. The opportunity was a great one to spread the word about walking football, the club in general and how being a member is not only good for the wellbeing of the individual but can offer a great community service too. Well done Pete!

# CHAPTER 20

# John Mulcahy

I started playing walking football in September 2015, and I have to thank Phil Andrews and the other players.

Phil kept asking me to attend one of the sessions he was arranging, and we used to meet at different parks in various locations in Northampton.

It helps us all to recapture our youth.

We meet at different parks, the Racecourse, Abington Park and Victoria Park to play games in the Town league and Sunday league. The club has grown from 5 or 6 players on some occasions to a membership of approximately 100 at Moulton Masters.

I had played football regularly Saturday and Sunday until about the age of 37. After I had retired I heard about Walking Football, and I have thoroughly enjoyed playing again. I have renewed old friendships and made many new friends.

We all have a love and enthusiasm for the beautiful game. Our Walking Football Club, the Masters, is affiliated to Moulton Football Club. Their nickname is the Magpies. Fortunately for us we have one of the best playing surfaces in the county. I, and other club members, help with the maintenance of the playing surface.

I get the same buzz going to a game of Walking Football as I used to when playing Saturdays and Sundays all those years ago. The social functions that have been organised by our Club Committee have been excellent! The day I decided to turn up at Beckets Park to play Walking Football has been one of the best decisions I have ever made. The camaraderie and banter with the other players is just great.

Finally, I want to pay a tribute to the late Billy Horne who used to play with us - his skills and friendship will never be forgotten.

# CHAPTER 21

# Glyn James

My story? Like many of us I had ongoing health issues and had to take ill health retirement because of stress, very high blood pressure and a couple of collapses.

I also had two operations for frozen shoulders, arthritis, etc, then Achilles operations on my feet, both cut and repaired. Finally the big toe on my right foot has metal work holding it together. So, as you can see, I have been in the wars like many of us.

I moved to Northampton almost 7 years ago and I saw a TV news items about Walking Football and thought, how good that looks and it could be just what I was looking for?

I was walking with my wife, Simone, across the Racecourse Park one day and stopped to talk to a guy who was running a Saturday football session for the kids there (little Messi's). I asked him if he knew of anyone who was organising Walking Football, and he said he had heard of something happening, but wasn't sure. This was 6 years ago now.

Simone will pick this story up later from her perspective. As for me, I found that Phil and a few others played at the Malcolm Arnold school on Monday nights. We were lucky if we had 10 to 12 turn up but found it we all really enjoyed it. Then as it grew bigger we started moving around the parks of Northampton during the daytime to meet others who were joining.

We then settled for Parklands Park and had met a few others who were playing at the sports centre by the Nationwide building. Things then got more interesting as the news was spreading by word of mouth leading to Phil booking Monday nights at Moulton school, and some days playing at the park. And the rest is history with our move to Moulton football club.

That is my history and what this has done for me is wonderful. My health improved almost immediately, not just the physical side but the mental side. I never thought I would play football again and enjoy it as I do. Friendships have been built and there have been laughs aplenty, which is great for the mind and the soul. I feel very lucky and happy that I have this in my life, and judging by the smiles on the faces of everyone else who has had, and still are having certain problems, I think that we all feel the same.

Hi readers, Simone here.

The same day when we returned from our walk from the Racecourse, I saw Phil's post on an online neighbourhood forum and made contact, because I knew how much Glyn had been yearning for something like this. Within a few days he started playing and he absolutely loves it.

He is happier because of it. And I, as a WF WAG, do of course have to play along and call him Harry Kane when he returns from a successful goal scoring spree, enduring his smug face and boyish smile.

In all seriousness though, physical and mental wellbeing are the core foundation of happiness and Walking Football has contributed so much to improving Glyn's and other people's lives. Long may it continue.

**Editor's footnote:**

The book will close with the clubs exploits at the 2021 Walking Football tournament hosted by Moulton FC during which Glyn was in scintillating form and finished as top scorer on the day, netting 7 goals in 5 games, resulting in our team picking up 'The Plate' Trophy.

# CHAPTER 22

# Martyn (Jaymo) James

I first joined this Walking Football group in September 2018 when they began playing at Moulton FC.

I'd known Phil Andrews for many years – since being teenagers in 'The Saddlers' and other hostelries around Northampton, but it was a chance meeting in the Grosvenor shopping centre in August 2018, when Phil told me about his involvement with Walking Football and the move to Moulton FC, that I decided to join. This was easily the best decision of my retirement.

During my first game there were about 14 of us, and when chatting after the game I realised that I had grown up in the same street, Ashburnham Road, as one of the other players, Dave Hetherington, who was a popular cornerstone of the club – so it is a very small world indeed.

Very quickly the club membership began to grow and team selection became more difficult as Phil, Dave H & Martin L tried to sort 30-40 guys into competitive match teams, a practise Phil referred to as trying to herd cats..!

Later Phil introduced pre-selection based on age and ability and emailed all members before each session advising what pitch they were on and what colours they would be wearing, and this proved to be a giant step forward as it meant none of our session time was being wasted.

The football itself is a great release as we see passion, commitment and very occasionally flashes of anger when decisions are deemed unfair, but the overriding factor is the sheer enjoyment of just being able to play football again.

When the games are finished, no one is criticised and players of all abilities are accepted and, somehow, we all manage to get along.

Whenever I say to people that I play Walking Football twice a week I don't think many of them realise the actual level of energy and drive needed just to complete 60 minutes of competitive sport. I often finish a session feeling absolutely knackered, but what a great feeling it is.

Well done, Phil and to all that assist in the running of this club – long may it continue...

# CHAPTER 23

# Dean (Deano) Barron

It was a bleak January day in 1959, Cottingham, Hull. I was born out of wedlock and in those days that was a scandalous event! The personal descriptive of my disposition has been addressed to me on many occasions but that is water off a duck's back, I am a Yorkshireman after all.

My first recollection of football and being mildly interested in the sport was of course the 1966 World Cup. At the tender age of seven I had my first flirtation with this fantastic pastime during this great event. It stirred within and fuelled my passion to want to exploit those skills and live the dreams which the game so vividly displayed. I was star-struck and watched in awe all that unfolded before me and which now engulfs, for those who are passionate, our whole being. I was on a mission; I set out to explore ways that me and me mates could perform our very own World Cup event.

Our home was a terraced house in a typical northern inner city street still suffering a second World War hangover. Thankfully, no outside privy, but the main garden feature was a bloody great 18 inch thick concrete air raid shelter that occupied 70% of the garden, and the rest was a patch of grass no bigger than ten foot square and bordered by Golden Rods, Gladioli and a Lilac tree; ergo: no space to play football!

The rears of the properties in Ryde Street were accessed via a strip of concrete known in Hull as a 'Tenfoot'. I will leave it to you, dear reader, to determine just why it is so called. Anyway, to me and me mates this space was the perfect area to create our pitch, our very own Wembley, and so it proved. There were many games, skills honed and demonstrated, victories, lifting of trophies, losses and injuries and of course many tears and falling out amongst so called friends. All in all, a good learning curve and character building stuff.

A progression of school, scout, and youth club teams followed by which time I had been introduced to being a supporter of a proper football team. You can blame my Uncle John for that fateful event. John had moved out to Leeds to seek his fortune and he treated me to a visit to Elland Road for my tenth birthday. We beat West Brom 2-1 on the day and the atmosphere was like nothing I'd ever experienced before. And so it stuck, even with the mighty Tigers being on my doorstep in my home town!

It was whilst playing with Hull Grammar under 15's that I was 'spotted' to play for the Hull Schools representative team. I stayed with this team up until the age of 17 and was representing the Hull Schools U19's.

We trained at Boothferry Park, the then home to Hull City and I guess you could call us the unofficial Hull City youth team. We didn't mix with the first team but we would bump into the odd player now and again and at least have a brief conversation. Players like Ken Wagstaff, Chris Chiltern, and Ken Houghton, who became the first Hull City youth team manager, would show a fleeting interest in our progression.

Ken Houghton was blessed with a pool of outstanding talent, with a number of lads who progressed well into the professional game, such names being:

- Brian Marwood (Hull City, Sheffield Wednesday, Arsenal and England)
- Noel Parkinson (Ipswich)
- Pat Heard (Everton, Aston Villa)

- Rob McDonald (Hull City, PSV Eindhoven, Besiktas, Newcastle, amongst others )
- Dean Barron (Bridlington Town)
- Others worthy of mention; Andy Jolliffe & Peter Jackson

No, I didn't quite hit the dizzy heights of some of my peer group who made football a lucrative career and fantastic lifestyle although things could have been rather different.

I put my direction in life down to meeting the love of my life, best friend, and soulmate of the last 45 years; Pat - Moll as I call her. But before I could 'claim her' as mine I had to fight off Brian Marwood's interest. How things could have been so different!

Married at 21, and our first born coming along when I was 24, my football career hit the buffers. Working through the week and then disappearing on a Saturday to play at such outback places like Guiseley Celtic, Garforth Miners and Emley Town required two evenings of training and full match day participation, with coach journeys in excess of three hours in some cases, which I hated as it made me feel travel sick. So it had to end even though the ten quid match fee would be badly missed.

I did actually return to play for Bridlington Town in 1987 at the age of 28 and to take a joint role as player secretary (the first and only in their history apparently) but we were soon to be moving out of Bridlington to Boston in Lincolnshire where I was to join Holbeach St. Marks playing in the local league. I kept that going until I turned 34 when it was time to hang up the boots. A few fun games of five-a-side ensued, but very infrequently. It was now time to spend time initiating my two boys into the great game that is football, something which rather sadly my father could not muster.

**Moulton Masters**

Getting to a certain age and being almost retired gets you thinking about many aspects of life going forward. One thing at the top of my agenda was my ability to hold a reasonable level of physical fitness within perspective.

Then you think of your mental fitness, the need to be regularly challenged and remain mentally agile and to think in a logical manner. Add the need of a reasonably diverse socially interactive environment into the mix and you have covered off a big chunk of consideration to keep oneself fairly active. What could possibly meet those criteria?

The answer, I believed, lay in football, the one comfort zone that is second nature to me. My age and lack of fitness suggested Walking Football, so I researched the local clubs in the Northampton area.

Unluckily for you guys I liked what I read about Moulton Masters and approached Phil. I was invited along for a 'trial'. I also thought this would be something that would suit my old mate, Mark Simpson, so we both rocked up for our first outing.

My time to date (4 years almost) with Moulton Masters would be best described as mixed. I've been banished from the club, selected to the committee, nominated as manager for the over 50's and 60's tournament squads and participated in refereeing on the odd occasion. My northern patronage is accepted/tolerated/abused in equal measure both on and off the pitch but hey, I always have the last laugh! Anyway I digress.

Phil introduced us and put us to task in a game and within minutes of the start, we had both received a blue card for inappropriate application! Welcome to Walking Football. Fall outs due to overzealous testosterone fuelled, and mistimed and misaligned tackling from behind got me into further trouble and I was expecting a bit of a reprimand for my misadventure!

It is great to see so many teams supported across the spectrum within our club, but for the life of me I don't understand how we have the majority of Loftus Road support within our ranks. Of course, we have Cobblers fans, MUFC, LFC, CFC, The Iron, even a Hull City fan, not to forget of course the mighty LUFC fans, oh and I nearly forgot, a Sheffield Wednesday token gesture. But to have 4 or 5 of our players supporting QPR? Do me a favour! Only joking guys 'don't lose yer Whippet'.

On a serious note, I am so grateful to each and every one of you for making Moulton Masters probably the best club of its kind in the country and for accepting me into the clan, warts and all.

Keep enjoying your football everyone, and remember to support your club mates -.always!

Hull Grammar under 15's circa 1974, Hull School's league champions.
I am back row 2nd from left next to future professional footballer,
Rob McDonald

Steve Batchelor

# CHAPTER 24

# Darren (Daz) Beerling

I love the beautiful game, but a glorious footy career has passed me by! I played (informally) in my youth and a coach fondly described my playing style as 'boundless enthusiasm masking a lack of natural ability'. Being born and raised in South Wales in the early 1980s in an era of amateur rugby dominance meant a succession of Welsh rugby internationals masquerading as PE teachers at my school ("take it easy boyo, teach the boys 2 days a week mush, nice an easy, then rest yourself for the game on Saturday bach"!) where football didn't feature on the curriculum, was never coached, openly discouraged – so I played with friends out of school.

I played again (informally) at university, scoring past the Rams' Peter Shilton in a student PR game before getting arrested with Mark Wright and Dean Saunders (a tale for another book)!

My glorious career was ended prematurely by a drunken parachute jump ("900 elephants, 900 elephants") from the rear door of a bus, hitting the kerb with my leg under the wheels!

After a decade out of the game I started playing weekly 5-a-side 'with work'. It was very enjoyable kicking my manager twice a week, but I lost my love for the game as I got older, as friends began bringing their quicker, fitter, more skilled sons along, and life, building a business and getting married got in the way of my glorious career! I stopped playing.

I discovered Walking Football in 2017. By luck. Maybe it was fate. I was battered and beaten physically and mentally after a horrific car smash, feeling isolated at home and in a dark place emotionally, unable to work, undergoing painful sessions to repair my body and cope with a traumatic brain injury, unable to do the things I once took for granted, fearing I'd never be given the OK to play footy again. Life got better when my postman, a Kettering FC fan and a witty conversationist willingly distracted from his daily post round, noticed my love of footy and invited me to a WF session at Kettering. I mocked his invite ("Geriatric footy? Get stuffed mate!") and repeatedly found excuses not to attend.

Hindsight suggests I was fearful and scared to play again, still in recovery and not yet ready to socialise, but fate dictated my physio sessions clashed with Kettering WF sessions but his perseverance led me to nervously joining in a Rushden & Diamonds session on Monday ("tell you what Daz, I'll meet you there, mate, don't let me down"!) despite him having no intention of meeting me there. It was his way of kicking me into action and breaking my cycle, but the genuine R&D warm welcome left its mark on me. I went back the following week, and the week after; lads messaged me when I missed a week to ask how I was, gave me lifts when I was too screwed up to drive, and before long I became a regular.

2020 saw me join Moulton Masters Fridays - a similarly welcoming and fun environment and I thank you and love you all. It's still a case of 'boundless enthusiasm masking a lack of natural ability' and I've still got no glorious career to reflect on. And I'm still unsure if I found Walking Football or if it found me! But what I am sure about is that Walking Football rescued me when I faced my darkest days, and there are many lads aged over 50 across Northamptonshire who have absolutely no idea how important their friendship and banter and post-match pints have been to my recovery. Just spending time on (and off) the pitch in their company has been a joyous godsend, and I thank all of you.

We have a saying in Wales 'Yma O Hyd' which loosely translates as 'despite all the odds we're still here', which is particularly poignant to me, but in many ways, sums up our Moulton Masters fraternity in general.

Diolch yr Fawr x

### Walking Football & Mental Health

It is widely recognised nowadays that regular exercise can improve a person's mental health as well as their physical well-being. One of the main benefits with playing football is the inter- action with other, like-minded, people – many of whom have had to contend with their own personal turmoil. It doesn't take long for bonds of friendship and mutual understanding to form and from this, a person's own self- worth will improve.

The Football Association have also been campaigning on behalf of mental health causes and club chairman, Phil Andrews, has contributed articles in support of this.

**Moulton Masters achievements and awards**

One big development of Walking Football in recent years is the growth of local tournaments which are often age group organised, to give all players an opportunity to represent their club. Although tournaments are always contested in a highly sportsmanlike manner, all teams want to win and the competitions sometimes become a little intense, but at the end of the day, we are all friends united in a common cause.

**Moulton Masters winners of Oundle Walking Football tournament 2019**

Team: Derek Ellis, Simon Elliott, Steve Griffin, John Richards, Ken Scott, Martin Wade, Phil Andrews, John Mulcahy, Martin Heasman, Derek Krajewski, Nick Kelk, Jim Ledington

**Moulton masters honours and achievements:**

Community Activity Winners 2019, Oundle 50s champions 2019, Moulton 65s Champions 2019 & 2021, Daventry Town 50s finalist 2021, Daventry Town 60s semi-finalist 2021, Northants County Cup finalists 2019

Internationals: Dave Poole (England) 4 caps to date

**Moulton Masters winners of the +65 inaugural tournament hosted by Moulton FC. October 2019**

The over 65s winning squad: Bruce Barnes, Jim Ledington, Steve Batchelor, Dave Poole, Phil Andrews, Ron Marzetti, Alan Dix, John Mulcahy

Great action shot as Steve Batchelor scores past Towcester goalkeeper, Chris Gedge on the way to Moulton Masters 65's becoming tournament winners

**They've only gone and won it again…**

Moulton Masters 65's team once again triumphed as Tournament winners in 2021

Team: Alan Dix Player/Manager), Dave Poole (hidden), Jim Cassidy, Paul Haynes, Ron Marzetti, Lionel Burton (captain) Ian Howells and Dave Cotton-Howells

Our all-conquering over 65's (blue) team continued their success from the 2019 event by retaining the trophy without conceding a single goal in any of their matches.

Of course, it does help having the England goalie, Dave Poole, in your side as he was once again in top form and unbeatable – even from the penalty spot.

Moulton Masters 65's won The Plate Trophy. Team:
Martin Wade (Manager), Martin James, Alec Wickert,
Dave Smith, Glyn James, Steve Batchelor, Mick Fisher,
Dave Hetherington, Dave, Robin Oakenfull

Moulton even had a third team in the tournament who also performed
well on the day: Team: John Thompson, Jim Rhodes, Glen Marriot,
Ron Birch, John Fitzhugh, Dave Trussler,
Front row: Dave Phillips, John Mulcahy, Steve Marshall

**Beginners Guide to Moulton Masters Walking Football Club**

If you wish to join us, please read the following. We shall also need .......

PERSONAL DETAILS:

Full name, Mobile, Email, DOB (some tournaments, including our own, are age-related), NoK and their contact number, a headshot picture (which we will usually take on your first session).

Also, for "marketing" (polite way of saying we like to be nosey!) we'd like to know where you heard about us please.

If you are a Facebook user – then please LIKE our page *@ WalkingFootballMoulton (currently we have 292 likes)*

Twitter – Follow us *@MastersMoulton*

Any medical conditions we should be aware of? These must be declared at any FA run tournaments

FEES: £15 annual membership due in August / September.

Subs: £3 for daytimes. Evenings are £4 (F/T), Unwaged or P/T are £3. If you are experiencing financial issues the club may be able to help. Contact Club Chairman (Pete Knight) directly or through Dave Conway (The Vice Chairman).

ATTENDANCE - we try to be as accommodating as possible to account for your holidays, work, medical condition, etc., but please be proactive in communicating with Phil who maintains the 'future attendance register' to plan for teams, pitches and referees. We run a system of *'expect me every week UNLESS I inform you'* - or *'DON'T expect me UNLESS I contact to - ask if there is a space'* – please never just turn up without agreement to play. This request became a rule since and due to Covid.

If you cannot make a session you're booked in for, then please send an apology – we understand there are work and family commitments and traffic! This is even more important with Track & Trace, as, if anything occurs we need to have 100% accuracy for the benefit of all.

Phil accepts written communication by Text, WhatsApp or email, so that accurate records are kept – please don't expect a verbal comment made to Phil to be remembered as he is about to kick- off, or getting into his car! Please give as much notice as possible (keep checking with your partner if you've any sessions you cannot make!). Please remember that the football is not so important as your wedding anniversary or her birthday!

COVID-19 Everyone must now give 'consent to play' by following this online link https://link.moultonfc.com/covid

**Editor's note:**

Although many of the Covid regulations have become more relaxed prior to publication the club remains very Covid aware and discourages too much close contact (no kissing the goal-scorer!) at present dressing rooms are still not yet in full use.

As a consequence of ongoing Governmental decisions regarding Covid restrictions many of the club rules will remain flexible and current status can easily be checked via the club website, or direct enquiries to club officials

PLAY – Even if you have played the game before elsewhere, or taken a break from us, please read all the below, understand and comply, as our rules and regulations will probably be different from others.

You must read and understand the FA Laws of the Game (LotG) which have been reproduced by the Club here.

Walking Football Rules Summary v1.1 Pat C

We use FA rules (as we are parented by an FA chartered club - formed in 1896 by the way!). We have added a couple of our own rules 'for safety' such as: we stop play for *'man down'* in case they've dropped glasses, hearing aids, false legs, taken a head knock or need medical aid, etc. Referee decides who restarts play.

YOUR KIT

You must only walk on the 3G surface (that's ALL the green stuff not just the actual pitch) to play, officiate or spectate, etc. in suitable footwear which is .... Artificial pitch boots, NOT Astros nor indoor flat soles shoes (as they flatten the grass) nor blades (can cause injury). So, don't listen to Sports Direct staff, listen to us!

These boots, in our youth, were known as 'moulded sole' - with 9 - 10 studs and are usually marked for Firm Ground or 'FG'. Never wear flat soled or SG (soft ground boots) or you'll incur the angst of many!

Current footwear is essential because we play on the best pitch in the County*. This cost £900,000; the green carpet is probably the most expensive in the town at £250k (not sure what that is per square metre) the rest was for the drainage and preparatory works). We need to keep wear and tear to a minimum so, likewise, do not place heavy bags on the pitches, and do not leave goals on thereafter sessions, either.

You'll see clubs, 'Goals' groups and councils who have not looked after their pitches when we visit them.

*Redwell, Wellingborough opened their beautiful new 3G facility in 2020 and these surfaces are the way forward. Kettering BC and other clubs are now looking into how they can raise the sums involved.

Boot Loans: We can loan a pair (sanitised) for the first 2-3 sessions until you're happy (and we are too!). Then please buy your own pair (Sondico are around £21 from JD Sports), these can be narrow fit so try Adidas (£30 upwards) and please return our loan pair clean! After each session, we ask you to loosely tie the laces together so we have pairs that are the same size.

Wear normal sportswear, appropriate to weather. We occasionally have rainwear, etc. for sale. At the beginning of 2021 the club altered the club badge to include the word "Masters" wrapped around the magpie. This will now be emblazoned on our new range of sports-wear.

Bibs – Previously we had coloured bibs provided mainly by the FA which were washed by volunteers. However, we did have two red and yellow ones bought out of the initial club funds. During Covid we currently cannot use these, so ALL players were told they must bring BOTH a white (not grey) and a very dark top. The annual membership fee would have been around £10 but we then decided to make it £15 and to include a White and Black bib to wear OVER any warm / rainwear jacket you wear.

Even if your team-sheet states which colour, you must please bring a change, in case we need to swap.

Gloves – These must be brought to sessions by anyone who is to play in Goal (or move kit). The club has loaned 10 pairs out to 'reserve keepers' for the duration of Covid-19. Ideally, every single player would bring their own pair, so we can all rotate, as pre-lockdown. Players can no longer just swap gloves amongst ourselves during a match to take a turn – it must be pre-planned but if there is a few days or week gap in between usage – this will be ok, if individuals are happy.

We can give you latex gloves to wear as glove inners, then share a pair on top.

Referee Whistles – Please offer to referee and bring your own whistle* if possible - Never swap whistles.

## MATCHDAY

Arrival / Dispersal Time – we must allow previous users (that's applicable on Mondays only) to clear the premises. No late arrivals, as the gates are now secured.

Current times are:

Monday: Arrive 6.55 KO 7.15-8.15pm

Tuesdays and Fridays: Arrive 9.40 for KO 10-11am

Bars: Depending on Covid tiering rules but usually open for around an hour afterwards (only if weather is OK to sit outside). This is what most of us look forward as much as playing - the chat and banter afterwards. It's great to socialise, deal with admin problems, even inter-personal disputes, referring decisions and of course update any future attendance issues with Phil.

Session Registration - You must be pre-registered to play that session and ensure the duty monitor (usually Dave H or Jaymo) records your attendance. You must show your subs, then put them in the open box. This must occur before you enter, and you must first use the hand sanitiser by the gate. There are extra sanitisers in each of the 3 'set up pitch bags'. You may be asked if you are free for the same session in the following weeks, a note may be made, but you must still text Phil. Please get into this proactive habit, as obviously he cannot chase all 100 players.

Referees – These players took and passed the FA Referees course: Phil, Dave Conway, Pat Curtis, Glyn James, Martin Littlemore, and Steve Batchelor. They have since passed on their knowledge and skills to others, some of whom have refereed FA or Sunday matches before, so we are fortunate in having some experience, please do not be shy to offer. The Referee list has now expanded to include Mark Simpson (now Ref guru), Dave Hetherington, Simon Elliott, Dean

Barron, Steve Griffiths, Jaymo, Dave Poole, Ed Hazelwood, Ron Birch, Steve Barrs, Richard Jobling, Tony Burwood, John Mulcahy, Scouse, John McMahon, Lionel Burton, John Austin, Alan Dix, Ron Marzetti). In fact, that's about half the club!

However, normally we only have refs when they are too injured to play, so if you become injured, and wish to remain involved with the club and give something back, then please offer to Phil to Ref - Mark S and / or Pat will then assist Our tournament refs have been praised by visiting teams and we've refereed at other tournaments, too, and even a couple at England trials for over 70s!

Spectators – None are allowed currently. However, if you wish to train on the pitch, you must advise Phil in advance, and only arrive and leave with other players.

Clubhouse and Changing Rooms – These are currently closed. You must therefore arrive changed, or change in your car, including boots (please do not use the steps to the pitch or benches to change boots or kit, as this causes bottlenecks).

Toilets – there is one available, access from the rear of the club in one of the changing rooms – you can access still wearing your studded boots. One in / One out system

Post-match social - we encourage all to stay for a cuppa (£1) or beer and chat.

Club donations – We are aware that some players wish to donate extra subs to the Club and this is appreciated as there was no income during lockdown. If you wish to donate, there are numerous ways such as 'buy a brick', advertising pitch-side boards, name on a seat (in new stand), raffle prizes, sponsor Race Nights etc.

New Guys – If you see anyone new, or on their own, please don't ignore them, have a chat. If you are new and feel you would like a buddy, tell me and I will find one. We have various sub-groups such as: Cobblers Fans (25 STH), Brixworth, Kingsthorpe, Keepers Union, Hard-rock, Quizzers, Race-Night goers, 'Coaches', we hold a Golf Day (at the Northamptonshire County Course in Chapel Brampton) and, despite all efforts to prevent it, we even have a 'QPR fans' group which is now 5-strong!

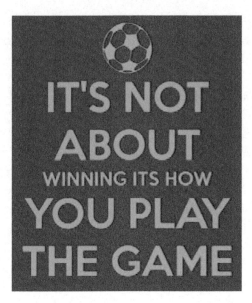

Typical session programme immediately post Covid, now, thankfully more relaxed, but at time of printing (November 2021) some restrictions still imposed

1. Whichever team, you're on, ensure there are no late changes and stick with that team for the session, including walking-on/off pitch. Take your water (and any bag) with you to your team 'break' place, so you don't mix with the opposition. .

2. You are responsible for your own warm-up (never stretch until you've warmed your muscles). Sadly, many fail to do this and pull a muscle (even on their debut and we never see them again). Maybe they overstretch?

3. Someone check boots of any new guys. You may be checked a few times – don't be annoyed – better safe than sorry. It's a £1/4million carpet!

4. Encourage your team mates to warm-up together, then conduct some ball-passing drills (some aren't as confident as others), discuss your team formation before KO. Do NOT warm-up with shooting practice, as you'll probably miss and your teammates will then have no ball to warm up with. You'll enjoy the game much more with some planning.

5. The Referee Briefing (note – remember the referee is always a volunteer, probably either injured or resting). It is disrespectful to talk during this, as your teammates may have a hearing impairment and so you, and they, may miss vital information. Refs will discuss with teams before KO any specific rules e.g.

   a. which touchlines are being used,

   b. prevalent rules.

   c. They may even remind all, or individuals who have a history of running or poor tackling.

   d. Referees will advise on 'water breaks' and take them only when the 'ball is dead' (to save arguments). No swapping ends after breaks to reduce chance of cross-contamination.

   e. FORMAT – To 'reduce exposure', rather than playing our usual 4-team 'round-robin' where you play everyone, we are temporarily halting that and just forming teams (bubble) and each team plays just one other team, this is 'in effect' your 'double-bubble'. The personnel in that group can be swapped around each week, and due to attendance there have to be minor tweaks each week. Eventually, we aim to return to 'round-robin' so that we all get to know each-other and have these mini-tournaments (plus we don't want any cliques forming or players to go stale). No one should be elitist or be looked down upon. Please, we accept banter of course, but no bullying. We have had a couple of instances to investigate and its never pleasant. If you feel your joke has backfired please be sensitive to the recipient and apologise.

   f. During play – we can expect to maintain a 1-2m social distance but we can try to not 'tight-mark', not breathe down opponents, not form 'defensive walls', and tackling from front-only is now allowed (there may be exceptions to certain players where there's no tackling, sometimes when a guy is new).

   g. Handball – Outfield players must not catch the ball or touch it, even at dead-ball situations – use feet only. Any cases of deliberate handball and even 'forgetting' must be penalised.

h. Covid-19 – To reduce airborne contamination risk, there should be no shouting, no spitting, no clearing of mouth and noses (even onto the ground) – please bring a tissue.

i. Dissent – There is absolutely no dissent to refs during or after a game – banter yes. Just accept their decision and play on, it's not the FA Cup, they may have seen something you haven't! Play to the whistle. Even experienced refs will make errors (but so will players!) as it's a very tough sport to ref, as you have to be close to see the contact, and far away to spot the running off the ball.

j. Claiming – we discourage 'claiming' for handball, overhead height, throws/corners, etc. - let the Ref make the call.

k. There may be 'marginal calls' such as overhead height, again let the Ref decide, not the players – and never catch the ball in-flight.

l. A referee will try and allow advantage to keep the game flowing but after 'that play' should advise a player they spotted their foul. Eight of us have passed an FA Ref course and we've then trained the rest! The Club will always support the Ref against any dissent. If there are issues these should be dealt with after the game and maybe later in the week, to allow parties to calm down and reflect.

m. The FA rules advise Referees that 'prevention is best'. So, if they see an imminent collision or the risks are increased as guys walk very fast, then they will call guys to stop or slow. It's much better to be safe than deal with an injury. This can be frustrating but again, this is for the long-term safety, and we shouldn't be over-competitive

n. ETHOS – Moulton Masters is football for all, so there is no elitism at this club. Help teammates to enjoy the game and include everyone. It's a team sport, not for you as an individual.

## CLUB KIT

1. Moulton Masters owns a variety of kit which is expensive (please respect this and offer to help cleaning and controlling it).

   a. Full strips for tournaments (2 x Black & White strips, Light Blue,

All Red and All Gold).
   b. Sets of Bibs x10 (Red, Green, Blue, Yellow, Orange). Do we need White and maybe Black next?
   c. Balls, Ball-bags.
   d. Medical and PPE kit
   e. Pump (and 4 spare valves!)
   f. Spare boots for new starters (size 5-12).
   g. Goalkeeper Gloves – 10 pairs are out on loan.

2. PITCH SET-UP GEAR (one Blue & Gold, we need two more as 2 are temporary Matalan carriers!)
   a. Rubber discs for goal areas
   b. Cones for touchlines
   c. Three x Elliott Mk2 "Golf ball on a bricked-rope" (Goal-area marker)
   d. Hand sanitiser
   e. Spare Goalkeeper gloves (hopefully)

The Kit Room is still currently out of bounds to all except Alan Sanders. He will move the 'set-up bag' to the rear door. Then volunteers are needed to move to their pitch, along with a bag of 3-4 balls. The kit should then be placed around your pitch as required (by those wearing gloves). Then post-match, each bag should be re-filled with the same items above and taken back to the rear door of the club. This should be an easy process, but it seems to be very difficult for some to grasp! Please can each team ensure all contents have been re-filled before you leave the pitch, as it's required for the next session and we do not want to spend hours having to re-check the contents. Use the Hand Sanitizer in the set up bag if required.

Some Hints and Tips –
   1. Listen to advice from others, they can help you enjoy the game more and prevent yourself from getting injuries.
   2. Skills – Pass to feet not to space to 'run into' – as obviously, you can't

run and you may decide to stretch – don't, as you will pull something! Just let the ball, roll past you, no-one will mind.

3. Short passes are more accurate, don't be ambitious.

4. Some rules are very similar to indoor 5-a-side because of the need to play safe, as in: no heading, no barging opponents, no entering keeper area, and also no Direct Free-kicks, no blasting ball at opponents (deflected goals are not allowed) and there's no offside. We use term 'not over-head height'. But some have still not grasped this, so here again, is the official explanation from our rules – *the whole of the ball must be over the top of the cross-bar for it to be 'too high'*.

5. Don't overstretch or 'go to ground' – no slide-tackles or slide-blocks. This is dangerous to yourself and opponents. You will be penalised.

6. Listen to Refs and discuss issues openly with them post-match so we all learn. Note: Mark Simpson and Pat Curtis are our Referee Guru and Rules Tsars.

7. First- Aid – If you are a First Responder, first aider (even if lapsed recently), ex-Fire & Rescue Chief, ex-Military, Police, Prison staff, etc. (so you're all trained) please advise Martin Littlemore. The defibrillator is behind the bar and we shall organise a demonstration at some time.

8. The sport has a system of blue cards (sin bins) and the club trialled this, to see that the effect was quite dramatic. We do not wish to re-introduce these, so simply obey the rules and no 'professionalism', delaying free kicks, etc.

Can I bring a friend – Yes, but you must inform Phil first, and provide some basic details. We like personal recommendation and we currently have space at all three sessions but we are desperately short of keepers (with own gloves) and referees. We shall rely on you to ensure your friend understands the rules and has read all the above.

We are the biggest club in the county, we have played on the best pitches in the county since it was opened (Aug 2018), we are in the top ten biggest clubs in UK and we've only been going 4 years from 4 guys and a dog on a car park, so it's been a remarkably quick growth. We're not perfect but we are striving to be. We'd like **everyone** to have an extra job in this club to contribute and share the workload – what's your job? We have Ref, Keeper, Pitch set-up / clear down, buddy for new guys..

Clubhouse has jobs for handyman, grass cutter, line-painter, then we've social organisers and fund-raisers. We also have a Golf-day. Oh yes, in 2019 we won the Daventry District community sporting award and a nomination at the Northamptonshire Community Club Awards.

## FINDING A CLUB
### *TAKING THAT FIRST STEP TO PLAY or HOW TO EXPAND YOUR CLUB!*

There are potential players out there who *want to find a club* and there are clubs out there who *want to find new players*. The quandary now is to ensure they all meet up! Here's some tips we've acquired over the past 5 years which might just help you all.

OK, so as a 'potential newbie', you last played football two, three, four decades ago? You absolutely loved it, and you wonder if you could recreate that 'feeling' that you just can't get from anything else? You've heard a little bit about this phrase 'Walking Football' (or maybe not) but you want to get fit (after an illness, heart attack, or just been shocked when you weighed yourself?); want to get out (maybe after redundancy, retirement or bereavement) and feel you should socialise - but have no idea how, where do you go? You have no dog and don't feel like walking solo around the park as it just reinforces your loneliness; you got a strange look (especially if you dared speak to someone else or were intimidated, you'd feel self-conscious?). Maybe, you don't know anyone to play squash or golf with, or it's just not your preference. Don't worry you're not alone – this guide can help you.

Only about five or six of our players watched the sport played on Barclays TV adverts (for digital awareness for the older generation) way back in 2013. Some have heard it mentioned on TV or local radio, by a broadcaster, or even a local MP, or you watched a demonstration at your local professional football club during the half-time interval (as our latest recruit did only last week) and then maybe it was debated in the sports bar afterwards?

Maybe you saw a poster in a newsagents, a corner shop, Doctors surgery, community centre, pub, café, barbers, sports centre, bowling club, parish magazine / notice board, a freebie 'trade-ad' or 'neighbourhood' magazine pushed through your letterbox, or there was 'a stall' at your supermarket (Morrisons, etc), village carnival, or a 'Silver Sunday event' (an open-day for activities aimed at the over 50s), even on a roundabout or you overheard it mentioned at a funeral!? A neighbour, or relative has suggested it to you? Some charities such as Age UK are getting on board, too, but with different degrees of success. All these do help but the best way for clubs to recruit is really through word of mouth from their existing players – nothing beats the personal touch; someone who has played who can answer all those questions and allay the fears that new (sometimes nervous) guys can have. All these have worked to gain a member.

Whatever it was, did you scribble down the contact number or email? Or did you take a photo with your digital camera on your smart phone?

If you're computer savvy, then the simplest way is to google the words *Walking Football near me* and suggested clubs will appear. But do their sessions suit your availability?

There are clubs on social media especially Facebook, many are under the umbrella of an organisation called WFA (Walking Football Association) who have a list of clubs. Often the best way, which not everyone realises, is to search your local County FA (Football Association) website, as they support the sport, and are taking more interest albeit at different rates across the country, which will list all walking football clubs who have registered their clubs. The FA should also help you set up your clubs by providing coloured bibs and balls.

Some of their websites are not always the easiest to navigate around but maybe someone could help you if you're struggling?

https://www.facebook.com/WalkingFootballMoulton

https://www.northamptonshirefa.com/players/ways-to-play/walking-football

https://www.northamptonshiresport.org/find-a-club/walking-football-northampton

https://www.moultonfc.co.uk/photos/walking-football--829417.html

https://www.facebook.com/search/top?q=walking%20football%20forum
https://thewfa.co.uk/directory/moulton-masters-northampton/

If you haven't got access to the internet through a computer or smart phone then ask a friend, relative or your local community staff to 'search' for a club. Still lost? Find any group of sporty guys, football fans at your local club and just ask them to help you, or ask a relative? Some professional teams, as well as amateur clubs, now have a Walking Football element.

Here in Northamptonshire there are WF clubs affiliated to Northampton Town Football Club, AFC Rushden & Diamonds, Corby Town, Daventry Town, Moulton FC, Crick FC, and Earls Barton FC. There are also teams affiliated to local sports centres in Northampton (Trilogy), Wellingborough, Towcester, Kettering, Desborough and new ones are just starting at Heyford FC, Silverstone and Rothwell. If you've an idea to set up a new group yourself or have a group of mates, I would suggest you approach an existing Football Club and see if they are open to the idea of adding a Walking Football element to their club. They might allow you to use their practice pitches (maybe its 3G so can play all year around), changing rooms, bar, clubhouse, first aid kit and the all-important defibrillator which can cost around £1000! Then there are the benefits that they can promote it to their supporters, ex-players and coaches. What's in it for them? Plenty! If they want more bar sales or are applying for grants from the lottery, FA or other sports and community funds, then having a WF element will only enhance that bid.

OK, you've now got a couple of numbers and contact names. Do you need to find a little courage to contact them? Are you going through those range of emotions that – this can't be any good, it'll be too slow, too pedestrian and have none of the sense of excitement you recall, or it'll be too quick and physical, and not consider your (*insert list of ailments here! ....... Dodgy* knees, bad back, high / low blood pressure, asthma, etc). Some guys were fearful that the game would be far too physical and could damage them. Be rest assured that all free kicks are indirect, so can't be blasted at you from 2-3 yards. Tackling should be *front on* or from *side* with no or minimal contact. Some defenders do get too close to attackers, some strikers do shield the ball by stepping back into the defender –

which happened first?

That's the referee's job to try and sort out. Quite often it is getting the right mindset into the players. There's no slide-tackling or deliberately 'going to ground' to intercept a pass. I used to love those tackles on a sodden pitch but from a safety point of view it's a very sensible idea now to stay on my feet.

**Don't forget these clubs are searching for new members and want you to contact them, but they don't know how to find you!**

There are just two hurdles for you to cross now – one, has your doctor given you advice to become more active or should you ask him if you're fit enough – as they always recommend you do when taking up any new physical activity; AND the other hurdle is to go along to watch the session. Some may not require you to make prior contact as they might be held on public facilities and have easy access to watch from the touchline, or through the chain-link fence – as ours used to be. Other sessions may be on private land owned by a school or an amateur football ground – as ours is now. and then you'll need an invitation – so give them a ring, send a text to the phone number or email them. I love getting those calls from newbies. If you get an invitation from an existing player, and your interest is piqued, then why not pop along - you might enjoy it just for the watching! We get guys who pop along just to watch, then stay for a chat with a coffee or beer. We get guys who only want to play in goal or referee – they can be your saviours to allow the rest of you to play outfield and safely!

I recommend that you always try and sample two or three different sessions to see what suits YOU best – I have played at around ten different sessions. Some clubs may only have evening sessions which suit the working, younger players and can be more physical and mobile. They might rock up at 5 minutes to Kick Off, then depart swiftly to go home for dinner. Which could suit you?

Whereas others play during the day and attract the retired guys who play at a slower pace and the pre-and post-match chat and refreshments are just as important as kicking the ball.

When we first started, we used to operate a 'turn up and play' system as we were just so glad to increase our numbers. However, when we started playing indoors or on fixed touchline pitches (often with fencing) we couldn't do this as we couldn't fit everyone on for safety. Now, players have to pre-book; however, that's not onerous, and it helps us. Once guys have played 2-3 sessions they know if they want to continue; most actually know before they even kick a ball that's it's for them and are chomping at the bit, but we take it steady. We now operate a system where we expect guys EVERY week unless then send me an apology to cancel. This means we can plan-ahead. With covid we had to know for *'track and trace'* exactly who was coming along. We've kept that system, so I now pre-select the teams and referees. Although this takes a lot of time to record, this means we can balance the players by numbers and each position. So, choosing teams doesn't eat into our pitch time and most importantly we're not waiting to see if 'a key' player 'x' (such as our best keeper, Derek) arrives at 2 minutes before KO, and we have to re-jig the teams about.

Now, most of our new guys are personal introductions from existing players, which is often best as they've explained the benefits, the rules, the ethos and help them settle in. For others it's a neighbour, a new mate, work colleague, or occasionally a former teammate from 40 years before. It's amazing how often (sometimes nervous) newbies arrive to the sight of friendly faces they last saw 'playing up the Rec', pushing kids around the park, down the shopping centre or DIY store or, dare I say, at a mutual friend's funeral.

My name, mobile and email is plastered over the internet, so I often get a call, text or email from someone seeking guidance as to whether this is for them. I'm always happy to chat through the positives and negatives but there is usually only one way to answer - come and along and see for yourself. We occasionally allow players to play straight off, or the last few minutes, especially if they've been playing 5 a side, veterans football or, indeed, play for another club. For the virgins, it's come along and take a look first, meet the guys and watch us.

We've usually two or three pitches of varying degrees of intensity so they can see there's a choice. Because we play on artificial turf (plastic grass with a rubber crumb to allow drainage) we need to wear the old moulded sole boots with short studs that we wore on hardened pitches in our youth in the summer. We have spares in every size, and we loan them out to newbies. The last thing we want is guys wasting money buying their own pairs and then finding they don't enjoy it (rare), or the old injury flares up (more likely) or they've bought the wrong sort of boot (occasionally).

When you do find an interested new player, I know it seems obvious, but get their contact details. So many times, especially in the early days when we were desperate to expand, our players have told me they've been chatting with this bloke down the pub: "I don't know his name, but he said he'd give you a call!" I say, "just pass him my number."

For safety, we don't let anyone play now without knowing their full name, mobile, email, Date of Birth, and, importantly, next of kin with their contact number. We had a guy on his third session who suffered a dislocated knee and I obviously needed to call his wife. I knew her (long story, but simply she'd played for us before he did). Anyway, she just thought this was typical of him to 'wind her up'; however, once a mutual friend came to pick her up, she realised this was real. Such injuries are extremely rare but being an ex-Scout, its best to 'Be Prepared'.

Living in Northamptonshire where Justin Edinburgh managed both The Cobblers and Rushden & Diamonds, we were shocked to hear of his death at a sports centre which incredibly had no defibrillator. Our club had one and this summer twenty of us attended a couple of sessions to be taught how to use it. In between these two sessions Christian Eriksen suffered his heart attack during the Euros 2021, which served as a salutary reminder. In fact, over the past six months, we've had four guys who have complained of chest problems at sessions, stopped and sought medical advice. Most of them have now had surgery with a stent or similar, and are now back playing and fitter than ever. One guy only believed the seriousness, when the ambulance arrived and insisted on taking him to A&E as he was having the heart attack at our session, but at the time he was presenting with what seemed like the symptoms of heat stroke (it was the hottest day of the year). He joked to the paramedics that 'the guys will be disappointed they couldn't try out the CPR and defib training on me'. He's a very fit seventy-three-year-old and has made his comeback playing again.

## THE DEBUT / FIRST SESSION
We always greet a new player with a warm welcome from the committee, and

our nice bunch of guys will make anyone feel welcome. We all tell them the same thing, which includes – *don't go thinking you're a 20-year-old chasing everything.* The famous quote is *'when (not 'if') a ball is passed too far in front of you, or too short, that you would normally 'run onto' it, remember you can't run, and then more importantly don't overstretch to reach it, as you'll pull a groin muscle and be out for 2-3 weeks!* We know it's sacrilege to watch a slightly mis-hit pass trickle over the touchline but please let it go. However, despite warming up, stretching, wear strappings and nearing the end of a session they all forget, do it, overstretch and regret it! What can we do? It's a topic debated at all clubs over the social media.

We ask everyone to declare if they have a medical condition that we should be aware of. Then after a couple of sessions we ensure everyone completes a registration to formally declare this, and record any ailments, conditions and medications. The paramedics have attended us once, and many other clubs, too, and they recommend this procedure so a copy can be taken with them if they take the casualty to A&E. We also charge an annual club membership fee which gives you benefits, third party insurance, a vote at the club and two free coloured bibs as well!

After the debut, a couple of sessions in, I get the confessions spilling out ... I've been meaning to come for weeks, months, or years, - why didn't I come before? this is fantastic - can I play every week?, can I register now? where do I buy my own boots?, how many times a week can I play? is there a tournament or league?

For others it's a slightly sadder tale of *'I've driven to the car park a few times but just couldn't get out of the car.'* I've had three guys couldn't even leave the house without me sending them a text full of encouragement and understanding. Yes, nerves, depression, low moods, fear of failure, whatever you call it – many of us have suffered and until you have, too, you can't explain it or help anyone else through it. We all know its 'stupid' but telling us that or 'stiff upper lip', 'chin up,' or even worse, 'man-up,' is exactly the wrong thing to say.

This is a summary of how our club (and others) has recruited its members over the past 5 years. We currently have risen to 115 active players, playing at least once a week, which has been a steady increase over time. We have some taking a break for assorted reasons – work, family, grandchildren, health conditions, niggling injuries, and weather. But we always try to stay connected as hopefully they'll return and bring friends.

## What's next?

One of the beauties of the sport is that as players get fitter and then have more free time, or retire from work, they then can play more sessions. However, it can be their club has no spaces, or more sessions to attend. Well, you are free to join another club. Even though I'm chairman of one, I have played for other local clubs because their sessions suited my timetable, and also because being just a member and no responsibility, means I can enjoy the session purely for the football and banter.

Occasionally, we play local teams in friendlies which can attract players from each other's teams to play in theirs. This can be viewed as 'poaching,' but with this sport the main point is all about the individual player and what they want.

We need our hardcore of members and want enough to continue playing each session. Yes, some teams are focused on leagues and cups and may poach a player for these. However, for us it's swings and roundabouts; we have had players turn out for the more competitive clubs in tournaments which is fine by us. Having players playing at more than one club really does promote us and help to standardise the rules in the local area, too.

## Secondary duties

In the military everyone who was an NCO or officer always had a secondary duty; I've borrowed that idea for the club. Now, many of us have a second job on a match day: we have a quartermaster looking after the kit, a squad of referees, sub-collectors, social / entertainments, fund-raisers, quiz masters, setting up / clearing down, first aiders, we even have five guys who help the club ground staff on another day to lay even more rubber crumb on the pitches, paint white lines and cut the grass on the grass pitches (it's a dream – playing with big boys toys - driving a tractor in the sunshine!) We also have a surveyor who will help next year when we need to turn some more fields into pitches, an architect, electrician, we even have a laundrette owner! At our last 65s tournament we even had 'youngsters' come along to help set up and act as ball-boys!

We have top blokes in our club, all helping each other on or off the pitch. The better players help the less able and the standard has really improved. Our more-able guys realise that without 'the others' there wouldn't be enough players to have a match, so they 'don't mind' our odd stray passes and routine wayward shots for the 'bigger picture'. At the end of the day, a shot is a shot, and the fact you have created a chance is normally enough. We are not that bothered about scores – well a couple are - and keep a record somewhere! But we get far more enjoyment about Joe's shot that trickled over the line, as he has the early onset of Parkinson's, rather than Fred who notched another hat-trick.

However, there has much to be said for Covid-19 in that we couldn't mix everyone up, so we stayed in our own bubbles of six. To do this we decided we'd keep the same six all evening playing against another six. Previously, we'd made four equal teams of mixed ability, and each would play each other in a round-robin, but now we don't do that. Instead, we have selected all the fitter guys onto one pitch and the less fit onto another. This has some advantages, as the latter now get far more time 'on the ball' and feel happier that they won't get 'closed down' so quickly, or tackled so hard. However, the downside is they don't get so much coaching to improve their own game. Hopefully, Covid permitting, we shall revert to some mid-way point where we can do both.

**Friendship Groups**

One of the great joys of the club is that new friendships are formed, or rekindled after decades, and it's a great feeling that the club has created these. I'm naturally interested in people and although I may not be that fanatical about certain things, like car engines or heavy metal rock, I know others are. So, we now have a group of 'head gaskets' and 'head-bangers' and hopefully we shall be able to socialise at a gig sometime.

It's at social functions that we're highly likely to recruit a new player because of his favourite band rather than his ability to 'thread a pass'! After one session at Malcolm Arnold Academy three of us retired to the local pub, for a post-session pint; incidentally the pub sadly has been a victim of lockdown, but has been a music haunt for years, so there was much to reminisce over. Two of the guys, co-founder Andy Clarke and newbie Glyn James, then got a bit competitive about a particular band and what their album titles were. Well, even I knew the first four were numbered sequentially and neither could recall the fifth one, and I looked on at their grimacing faces - this was typical 'man-behaviour' of trying to guess random facts which are getting more difficulty as senility descends upon us all. Amusingly for me, I, as a former quizmaster who didn't know the albums, did actually know the answer. So, I departed for the loo saying I'm just going to visit the *'House of the Holy'*, cue derision. When I returned, they were still at it! One was sure he was more of a fan than the other until Glyn rolled up his sleeve to display *'Led Zeppelin'* tattooed up his forearm – trumped I'd say! - and there aren't many tattoos amongst our age group, either.

Of course, the one time I had left a CD in my car boot after 'a date' I got ridiculed for my taste, and I'm still the only one who will admit to being in the 'Harold Melvin and the Bluenotes' fan club!

### Kingsthorpe Mafia

Then we have a group of guys from Kingsthorpe, which is a huge area on the northern side of town, and which has a unique feel to it. So, we have the Kingsthorpe-mafia who chat after sessions together, reminiscing about the local pubs, shops and characters.

### Boy Scouts

One of the earliest recruits was a guy I saw up the Cobblers, but I really knew him because 45 years before we'd been in the scouts together. Another guy joined and we recognised him, not from just the boy scouts, but from the 'gang show' as well. Then another joined and I must say they are great at taking responsibility, taking initiative, taking subs, setting up the pitches – a bit like camping really? I read once that a high proportion of US astronauts had been Boy Scouts, so if ever we decided on some space exploration, we have the right team amongst us. Recently, a 70-year-old guy joined whose surname was synonymous with local scouting – so we asked Dave Shrewsbury if he was a relation, and he was the son of. So this prompted an exchange of photos, articles, and chat about the annual camping competition, The Thornton Trophy. We have enough for one patrol.

After scouts I joined up into the Army - similar, just more maps and camping really. Now our club has had six ex-servicemen, again 'good sorts' who know how to rub along with anyone, and will play any sport regardless of ability – just for the banter. We've also got three ex-police, two ex-fireman and, importantly now, a First Responder, Graham Clarke, and Charlie O'Neil, an ex-paramedic who could be more vital bearing in mind that some of us have reached a certain age. One day, we'll all turn up in uniform and perform some drill?

### The rest

Over the years we've had over 200 members play for us, but we've had guys leave when we moved location, and they preferred playing at that venue, or that size pitch, or with those players. We've had guys travelling long distances to us until clubs were formed more locally to them; some came to play after work then travelled a long way home, but the increase of homeworking has affected that. We have moved across the town to play whenever a suitable venue arose, but we always seemed to 'home' back to the same part of our town. Now, I can't see us ever leaving.

### Moulton Masters steering committee:

Chairman: Phil Andrews
Vice-Chair Moulton FC (parent Club) Dave Conway
(Responsible for Walking Football)
Registration & membership: Martin Littlemore & Lionel Burton
Rules & Referees: Pat Curtis and Mark Simpson
First aiders: Dave Webb, Dave Roberts, Terry Marconi,
Graham Clark (first responder), Charlie O'Neil
Subs & Laundry: Dave Hetherington & Martin James
Entertainment's officer: Martin Littlemore (& support)
Tournament Organisers (away): 50/60s/PDFL: Dean Barron,
over 65's: Alan Dix, over 70's: Lionel Burton

## REFLECTIONS BY PHIL ANDREWS

My co-editor is now pressing me for my 'final piece'. It has been quite humbling to read all the accounts of the players who have joined us. I wonder what would have happened if I hadn't received life-changing injuries way back in 2007? Would I have still been playing 'ordinary' football past fifty and beyond with the younger work colleagues? Possibly. But probably not. I think I would have stumbled across this great sport anyway and chosen the same club ethos of everyone welcome – 'football for all'.

Not all clubs are formed the same way. Some Walking Football clubs have been formed by a group of ex-players from very successful amateur or semi-pro teams who wanted to re-kindle that adventure of playing at the highest levels possible, winning cups, medals, travelling all over the UK and into Europe to play in tournaments, and some players even gaining regional and international attention – which is a great motivation for them. However, for me, who couldn't get in the school team, who'd never had any coaching until he was thirty and then in the Army, it was all about just the fun of a match, and 'looking after the guys like me', who didn't make the first eleven, who were left behind at barracks whilst the top players had a Wednesday afternoon sports match, and ostensibly those who just 'couldn't play anywhere else'. In fact, when I started the club that was one of my key criteria – I couldn't play anywhere else, nor could the others, so everyone had to fit into that ethos. This club was first and foremost for those who loved playing for the camaraderie of the whole club, not the individual.

I had few grandiose ideas back six years ago, when there was just 6-7 of us, that we were going to start exceeding 14-18 at a session and need a bigger pitch. I did, however, think it would be perfect if there was a session every day somewhere locally, so that if you couldn't make it one day, they'd be another opportunity somewhere else, and you weren't waiting for next week to come around.

At our club now, we have around ten of us who come along to every session, but as the matches have become a little quicker and we've aged and incurred a few muscles strains, then, we've unfortunately not been able to play at them all. However, we enjoy the 'club atmosphere' so much that we come along to help set-up, 'to make up the numbers' or we play in goal, or referee or just spectate (even chat to the goalkeepers!) and we stay behind for a cuppa. Friends, parents, sons, daughters, and grandchildren have all come along to *see what grandad's up to.*

When we returned after the first Covid lockdown there was a marked increase in attendances at all sessions and the number of sessions – as guys wanted to get out, regain their fitness, play more often (because they might have been furloughed, or working from home and escaped to us in their lunchbreaks) and many realised then just how important the club was to their mental, as well as physical, health. Our numbers then contracted, as we could go away on holidays, see families, and it was difficult to plan the sessions as folk would often send 'apologies' with little notice.

Now as we pass the end of summer holidays in 2021 there are another batch of newcomers who have discovered us, have free time and are looking to fill their days – oh to be those people again, looking in wonder as they go through the range of emotions that we all did at the start – will I be fit enough, will the old injury flare up again, will I know anyone? But for most of us, this is sport as good as I remember it when I played from dawn to dusk as a kid.

Surely, football with no running, isn't football? Well, come along because fortunately tens of thousands have found their local clubs and popped along see which one will suit them – indoors, outdoors, grass, 3G, 5 a-side, 8 or 9 a-side mixed, ladies – maybe a mixture of them all on a different day of the week!?

BBC Reporter, Helen Blaby, interviews Phil Andrews with fellow walking footballers Martin Littlemore and Linda.

**The price of fame, publicity, and the media! (Community)**

The increase in popularity over the last few years has seen some media interest descend upon us and we've been very happy to promote the sport locally and nationally.

Having a vibrant university in the town, there's been a few occasions where the Head of Media or Sports has suggested to their students that we'd be an excellent pet-project for a thesis or journalistic piece. So, we've been delighted to help students by inviting them along to sessions and experience the atmosphere. Depending on which angle they are looking for, we have a few players who are happy to speak on camera and be interviewed on generally *what health benefits has Walking Football brought for you.'* The local BBC and independent Radio broadcasters have invited us along to their Sports show and now I've carved out a media carer for myself! I've been on the front cover of a university magazine, appeared on local radio shows including Inspiration FM where the young DJ Ryan was a son of one of our players, Rob Leivers, and BBC Radio Northampton phone-ins during lockdowns.

We've also managed to get Local BBC Radio presenter, Bernie Keith, to ring up a couple of our players with 'bouquet requests' – when one of our most hard-working clubmen, Martin Littlemore, was feeling a bit low and needed a lift, and the other, Dave Poole, to congratulate him on winning his first England call at the age of seventy.

When Dave's wife passed him the phone little did Bernie know that Dave was taking an early morning bath to help relieve the bumps and bruises of the day before.

For the students we shall be looking out for the names Dayna Richman et al to see if their media career was built on a solid foundation made at our club!

The boot was on the other foot when we got a call from the UoN on another matter - this time they wanted us as students! Well, as guineapigs really. Brett Baxter was doing his BSc (Hons) and conducting a study on 'falls prevention in the elderly.' This is a major concern for the NHS as so many elderly patients fall, break a limb, and suffer badly with rehabilitation. So, four of us attended weekly 'strength-monitoring' classes to gauge our levels of balance under scientific conditions. These found our weekly football exercise was having a positive effect on our balance and strength. Hopefully, the findings will someday help save someone and get strength testing apparatus into community centres, etc. Certainly, I'd have to say I'm much fitter than I was six years ago and I'm sure most of my fellow teammates would agree about themselves.

Another, venture saw one of our players, Alan Miles, aged seventy-one, declare he was also a Disc Jockey at local Radio NLive (106.9FM or online). He hosts a weekly musical extravaganza on a Thursday evening, where he interviews a notable town personality (plus me!) whilst playing their chosen records – a sort of desert island discs. So, a comfortable two-hour show was recorded live in NLive, which was heard by a few people I'm told! However, someone who did hear it was prompted to ring in and has joined us! I was pleased to discover that Alan now hosts a Sunday morning Breakfast Show from 7-8am, too. Maybe he'll invite me back?

I don't get embarrassed when being interviewed (not since war correspondent, Kate Adie, first interviewed me abroad once!) and maybe my record choice was a little bit suspicious to some, but Alan and I had great fun!

A couple of players attended the annual BBC Big Health drive at the Northamptonshire Cricket Club (Wantage Road) and spoke live on air with Helen Blaby, and we also managed to find a couple of players there, too.

One day I was rung-up and asked if we'd like to help our local dementia group at their weekly meet-up as they were trying out different activities with them. I was inundated with offers to help, so eight of us met up. The exact location was kept secret until the day before, when we were delighted to set-up a pitch, and kick a ball around with the group – in a library! Fifty years ago I'd have been told off (well shushed) by a haughty librarian for dropping my ball on the wooden floorboards, but now I was being encouraged to kick one around and make as much noise as I could – how the world changes! Many goals were scored and both sides celebrated when the ball went in either goal – no matter which end – who cares! There was much joy with the goal celebrations, too, and was a fantastic hour or so. Afterwards we chatted to all, and a couple of the relatives came along in the following months to play with us, which served a purpose as respite care for them. Sadly they had to give up Walking Football as they were too busy caring full-time for their partner / parent.

Our local Moulton Village holds an annual Carnival and a Silver Sunday which has given us more opportunities to present ourselves to the local fraternity. The latter is an event aimed at the over-fifties to get involved in local activities through the community centre. We have an excellent rapport with them and once a couple of guys turned up to watch us saying they asked the community helpers if there was a ping-pong table somewhere for a game ....and they'd been re-directed to us! – both joined us! I never did discover if they found their ping-pong table.

Each year we hold a MacMillan coffee-morning, and someone will bring cakes. Martin Littlemore loves baking. but one year Dave H stated that he could surpass Martin's efforts, so he 'paraded in' with his tray covered by a teacloth and did the 'big reveal.' As we gazed upon the beautifully decorated and brightly coloured pink, yellow, and chocolate coloured fondant cakes – and yes, he said 'I made the paper cups too' – well done Mr Kipling.

This year, one of the wives, Shan Goodridge, brought her cakes to all three weekly sessions – and raised over £300 for the local cancer hospice - Cynthia Spencer. The next week our hairy Canadian player (former Ice-hockey goalie) raised £500 for his *brave the shave,* also in aid of MacMillan cancer research.

**We've even had players taking advertising hoardings at Moulton FC to help publicise our team:**

We've held a couple of club fund-raising events at the club too, but just as we were getting into the swing, Covid struck and so we shall need to build that side up again, not least because it was a heavy financial burden for many clubs with costs still to pay, but no income. Fortunately, the grassroots kids' teams still paid subs, we collected subs when we played up the park for free, and donated these. We're also holding a quiz night which we hope will raise over £300.

Our members also stated that the costs of subs was 'too cheap' in comparison to other sports so we increased subs by a £1 to £3, and this will raise another £70-£80 per week or £3,500-£4000 a year. If anyone wants to donate some funds to help with our 'running costs', please contact me at the club! Our beautiful pitch cost £250,000 and should last us 10 years, so we need to raise £25k per year just for that! However, with excellent grounds-maintenance, and ensuring we reduce wear and tear by wearing the correct boots, etc. hopefully we can extend its life and reduce the annual cost. Other clubs at Kettering and Earls Barton, I hear, are now looking at a similar facility. It certainly is the way to go, and matches up to Tier 5 (The National League) can be played here. However, as Harrogate Town and Sutton United know, you can't use them in the Top 4 Tiers of the English game, although bizarrely you can in the European Competitions. England lost to Russia on one way back in 2007! Now there is a hybrid version which could be the way forward?

I'm active on social media, mainly Facebook, though we have dabbled with Instagram and Twitter; anything to spread the word around about this sport. It works, as many guys have seen it mentioned there a couple of times (or their families have) and got in touch.

Certainly, one of 'Red Letter' days for me was opening a letter from the local council informing us that our club had been nominated for a community sports award.

Eight of us made the short trip to Daventry where we dined on takeaway fish 'n' chips and beer. The event took a dramatic turn when we were announced as the winners in our category, and were presented with a certificate and a shield. Then we learnt we'd made it through to the county finals, and despite a better venue (Park Hotel by Radisson) and food, we became one of the runners-up, but still feel mildly shocked about it.

Another time we managed to enter a county-wide competition called the 'FA People's County Cup' at "Goals" - the venue is owned by a national company who run outdoor 3G centres with multiple pitches. We had entered six 5 a-side teams from our group and arrived to find just seven other opponents, and three of these weren't even from our county but were allowed to side-step the 'County' rules! Although the competition and the venue (with the floorboards which speeded up the game from the walking pace to running) were good, unfortunately, it wasn't the best organised event (no-one knew the scores or the league table – so our semi-final opponents from Leicester had showered, changed and were just leaving the venue, when they were asked to play us – which they refused – so we had a long gap of an hour before the final) and it put off some of our players from ever competing again. However, I did manage to find myself being totally blindsided by being 'called out' by the FA representative (Tony Major) to receive an FA county volunteer of the year award. Although thinking back, by managing to enter all the names of my forty competitors in the correct teams on the 'Goals' complicated computer system, I deserved something higher really - a Nobel Prize maybe?

**Any Ex-pros play?** A question I'm often asked, and the answer is yes, one of my first ever stories I was told was about a chap who was on holiday in Portugal with some mates and they'd entered a Walking Football competition out there. Much to their surprise they reached the final and they tentatively took their places on the pitch where a crowd had gathered to watch them play against a team called Sheffield Hallam. So, this chap lines up to see what shape the opponent is from the kick-off and thinks, 'that guy is a dead-ringer for .... Oh! It is, I'm pitched up against Chris Waddle. Chris Waddle quote from WFA website May 2020: *I've started playing Walking Football which I enjoy, although the amount of time you want to run with the ball, it's so frustrating. I'd love to play one more year and after that its Walking Football for the future.*

Phil Neal, of course a local Northampton boy and hero to many at our club, plays for Knowsley WFC alongside Alan Kennedy who was selected to play in an England over sixties team alongside Tommy Charlton. There's a quiz question – what age was the eldest Charlton brother when he last played for England – the answer was Jackie Charlton, aged an amazing thirty-five. Now that honour has been bestowed on Tommy Charlton, aged seventy-three!

I'm told there's an Aston Villa team of ex-pros from their 1981 European Cup squad, and I've heard of many others from all the national football leagues.

At Northampton Town our all-time Manager hero is Dave Bowen who also played for the club, as well as captaining Arsenal, and then Wales, in the 1958 world cup but, most-spectacularly, managing The Cobblers when they achieved the then record feat of promotions from tier four to tier one for our only season in their 125-year existence. His son then played for the Cobblers for 5 years, scoring 24 in 65 before a transfer to Brentford, then Colchester, where he suffered a serious car crash which put him out of the professional game. However, aged sixty-one he made a comeback with us for a couple of sessions at Moulton Masters before the old injury played up again, it was nice to play on the same pitch as him, though. Despite invitations to ex-Cobblers players that we meet up at Sixfields on matchdays, we have yet to persuade another ex-professional to turn up.

So, to all those guys who turned us down we say, 'well if it's good enough for multi-award-winning England International Phil Neal, then maybe there's something you're missing!

### It's a Team effort

Although, I get much of the plaudits, (including occasional 'telling's off' from the parent club chairman for misdemeanours by members). You cannot run any organisations like this without the support of a good team behind or preferably with you! In the early days when we had around twenty, I would make the 'availability calls', book the pitch, collect subs, choose teams, distribute bibs, buy 'pop-up' goals – then carry them to and from my car. You ask guys to help but nothing beats a guy offering to help. So, now I can relax, turn up late, or even not attend at all (holidays or sick) knowing that everything will run like clockwork. Whenever, there's a new guy join I wonder what other non-playing skill he'll bring. Like Mark Simpson who has taken our refereeing to a much higher standard than I could ever dream of! Or guys who look after the subs and kit as though it's their own. We wanted a first aider - now we have six, plus an ex-paramedic at one session and a first responder at another, with the possibility of a GP joining us soon! With our ailments we need all the medical help we can get.

We have guys who run summer tournaments in kids' soccer and now can enjoy this throughout the year; guys who can and want to referee; guys who love to arrange socials, golf-days, foot-golf, and quizzes. We have others who are already planning car treasure hunts, darts / pool nights, clay-pigeon shooting, kayaking down the River Wye and outward bound in North Wales with a former paratrooper! Then we have Stuart Fraser who produces amazing photos and videos, who etched the sizes on the soles of our spare boots, provides power sources for events, is a carpenter, model maker and evens owns a laundrette for our kit!

### A jigsaw of players.

So, we not only have twenty-five season ticket holders at Northampton Town FC, but we've now got fans of Stoke, Sheffield Wednesday, Leeds, Hull, Nottingham Forest and Notts County, Reading, Cambridge United, Scunthorpe United, Carlisle plus a smattering of Premiership clubs of course, but somehow, we've allowed four or five fans from Queens Park Rangers fans to join us!

### FINAL PIECE

What of those original five you ask? Well Andy Clarke aged seventy-three emigrated to the Peebles area and we know he has turned out for a team in Edinburgh. Andy Roberts, Craig Pittam and Stuart White all still play when shifts allow. Gnasher the dog is now quite old and poorly, but his dad, Chris Gedge, promises he will return to us at some time. What about me, I almost forgot to include myself, but after the life-altering event of 2007, loss of job, 1000s of hours of rehab, court case, divorces, etc., I am so relieved I discovered this sport. Unwittingly, it has given me a new drive and enthusiasm for life. It's now my 'retirement job; OK I'm fortunate that the Court case provided me with a financial sum to fall back on, but money isn't everything - you need a drive and a purpose, and the club has given me that. Its saved me for mental anguish and given me a new goal for maintaining my physical health, too. Mostly it brought us all new friends.

You've read the others' stories herein and it's clear that this sport is filling a gap in the lives of so many similar folks to myself.

What of the club? What's next? We currently play for an hour on both a Tuesday and Friday morning and if the festive dates fall right, it's not unusual for us to play every week of the fifty-two per year! We certainly have the space to expand on weekday daytimes to an almost infinite level, as its rare our venue is booked for more than our 2 hours a week, and a couple of hours for the local NTFC academy. So, in theory another 40 hours' worth of Walking Football could be held!! So, next year will we be either expanding our current hour session or adding a new weekday? But with that will come a greater new commitment from all the organisers.

We also play on a Monday evening which attracts the younger guys still working, but expansion is difficult, so we're stuck around the sixty-membership mark (56 players, that's eight teams of 7 a-side, plus four referees).

Weekday evenings and weekends are in demand for the rest of the club to run their training sessions. These times are booked solid from groups aged 5 years up to adult men and ladies during the 'usual' football season of September to early May. We also have twelve names of guys aged in their forties who'd love to come and try the sport and we even have organisers for that, but no hour spare for them to play. That's a shame as they could be our 'youth development squad' for the future! We shall have to wait and see how this dilemma unfolds.

Printed in Great Britain
by Amazon

10074549R00079